THE MARKETING ECHO

NAVNISH BHARDWAJ

Navnish Bhardwaj
1st Edition

Publication Date: September 2025
Price: ₹ 349 / $ 10
ISBN: 978-93-7164-822-6
Published by:
Adhyyan Books
Office No. 589,
Opposite Vivanta by Taj,
DDA SFS. Pocket-1, Dwarka,
Sec-22, New Delhi-110077
Website: http://adhyyanbooks.com
E-mail: contact@adhyyanbooks.com

Printed at: Repro Printers, Delhi

FOREWORD

Today's hyper-connected, content-heavy world, being seen is no longer enough. The real challenge for brands is to be remembered, trusted, and ultimately, chosen.

This book doesn't just tell you what good marketing looks like, it shows you how to embed your brand into the minds of your audience through a repeatable, measurable process.

Whether you're a founder looking to carve out a niche, a marketer striving to make your brand stand out, or a strategist aiming to build long-term category dominance, this book will challenge you to think bigger and echo louder.

It's not just about existing in the market. It's about owning the narrative. And "The Marketing Echo" shows you how to do exactly that.

— Parul Mehta Bhargava

CEO @ vCommission

PREFACE

I wrote this book because I was tired of seeing brilliant businesses go unnoticed while louder, less capable ones owned the conversation.

The truth? In marketing, it's not just what you say... it's how often, where, and how consistently you say it. Repetition breeds familiarity. Familiarity breeds trust. And trust leads to dominance.

This book is a guide for marketers, founders, and business leaders who want more than growth, they want ownership of their market.

You'll find actionable strategies, psychological insights, and real-world case studies that show how brands embed their message so deeply into the market that they become undeniable.

— Navnish Bhardwaj

ACKNOWLEDGEMENT

Writing this book has been a journey of reflection, learning, and deep gratitude.

First, to every mentor, colleague, and client who challenged me to think bigger, thank you. You shaped the strategist in me.

To the marketing teams I've worked with, you were the real battlefield. Your wins, struggles, and hustle inspired the frameworks in this book.

Special thanks to my family and close friends for your unwavering support. Your belief in me has been louder than my doubts.

Lastly, to every reader picking up this book, you're not just reading a book, you're stepping into a strategy. May you use it to dominate your category and echo louder than the noise.

CONTENTS

1

THE POWER OF THE ECHO – HOW SOME BRANDS BECOME UNSHAKABLE

HOW SOME BRANDS BECOME UNSHAKABLE

In 1997, Apple was dying.

The once-revolutionary computer corporation was on life support with a barely 4% market share and less than 90 days from insolvency. The world had written Apple's obituary. The press called it a "has-been." Competitors waited like vultures to pick apart whatever remained of its dwindling market position.

Then Steve Jobs returned. And with him came what might be the most powerful example of market psychology ever deployed in modern business.

It wasn't a new product. It wasn't a revolutionary technology. It wasn't even a groundbreaking business model.

It was a message. A message so powerful and delivered with such unwavering consistency that it rewired how an entire generation perceived not just Apple, but creativity, innovation, and their own identity.

"Think Different."

Two words that would transform a nearly bankrupt computer manufacturer into what would eventually become the world's first trillion-dollar company.

But why? Why did these two words, combined with black-and-white photos of rebels, artists, and disruptors, succeed where billions of R&D and marketing by other firms failed?

The reason is in what I refer to as **The Echo** a psychological effect where repeated, consistent communication builds an impenetrable reality in the minds of consumers. When deployed correctly, The Echo doesn't just influence what people buy. It changes how they think.

In the chapters that follow, we'll break down this potent psychological force not simply as an intriguing theory, but as a manipulable formula that any company, small or large, in any industry, can use to engineer market supremacy. You'll see why some brands engender rabid devotion and others are mere interchangeable goods. Most importantly, you'll understand how to make your own brand go from forgettable to unbreakable.

THE BIRTH OF AN UNSHAKABLE BRAND

Apple lacked ground-breaking new products when Jobs introduced the "Think Different" campaign. Still on the drawing board were the vivid iMacs. The iPod was years away. The iPhone wasn't even a concept.

What Apple had was a story. A narrative so compelling and delivered with such relentless consistency that it began to echo in the consciousness of its audience.

The commercial's words still resonate today:

*"To the crazy ones. The misfits. The rebels. The troublemakers. The round pegs in square holes. The ones who see differently. They don't like rules. They also question the current state of affairs. You could cite them, dispute with them, compliment or condemn them. Ignoring them is the one thing you cannot do. since they bring about changes. They lead the human race forward. We see them as geniuses even though some of you would deem them crazy. The ones who act are the ones who are crazy enough to believe they can change the world.

This wasn't just advertising. It was identity formation. Apple wasn't selling computers. It was selling belonging. Purpose. Self-concept. It was creating a psychological framework where choosing Apple wasn't just a purchase decision it was a statement about who you were as a person.

But the genius wasn't just in the message itself. It was in how the message was deployed.

The "Think Different" campaign appeared everywhere billboards, magazines, television, store displays. It wasn't just consistent in frequency, but in execution. The black-and-white aesthetic. The rebels and visionaries. The simple, powerful phrase. Every manifestation of the brand reinforced the same core identity.

From 1997 to 2002, Apple hammered this message with unwavering discipline. The market's perception shifted not because Apple told people once that they were innovative, but because they repeated it thousands of times, in thousands of ways, without deviation. When competitors changed messaging with market trends, Apple maintained course.

This is the first law of The Echo: Consistency creates reality.

THE NEUROSCIENCE OF BRAND STICKINESS

To grasp why The Echo is so effective, we must look at how our brains process information and create beliefs.

Though it can only take in roughly 50 bits, the human brain must cope with roughly 11 million bits of information every second. Our unconscious filters 99.9995% of all we hear. Brands are competing in this sea of information for a tiny fraction of conscious attention.

Our brains use a mental shortcut called the "availability heuristic" to determine what's important. Simply put: the more frequently we encounter something, the more important our brain assumes it must be. This is why political campaigns, religious teachings, and cultural norms all rely on repetition not because people are forgetful, but because repetition literally rewires neural pathways.

This explains why repeatedly seeing the same brand message doesn't just increase familiarity it literally changes how our brain values the information. When we see "Think Different" for the hundredth time, our brain doesn't just recognize it, it assigns its greater importance than information we've encountered only once.

In a groundbreaking 2001 report in the Journal of Consumer Research, people tended to rate reheard claims they'd heard lots of times as more probable to be true than new claim seven if told explicitly that those repeated claims were untrue. By using fMRI imaging to explore this phenomenon, researchers found activity decreased in the areas involved with critical thinking when things were reheard and was boosted in areas involved with feeling familiar and assessment of truth.

This psychological phenomenon, the "illusion of truth effect," explains why repetition is not simply a marketing strategy it is an effect reality-creating force that functions below the level of conscious thinking.

But Apple's execution of The Echo went deeper. By consistently associating their brand with revolutionary figures like Einstein, Gandhi, and Dylan, they created what neuropsychologists call "neural coupling" the brain begins to associate the emotions and attributes of one concept with another through repeated pairing. This is the same mechanism that allows Coca-Cola to "own" the feeling of happiness or Nike to claim the emotion of athletic achievement.

After enough repetition, our brain literally can't think about "innovation" without triggering neural pathways connected to "Apple." This association becomes so entrenched that it resists contradictory evidence even when competitors introduce more innovative features, our perception still assigns the "innovation" attribute to Apple.

This is the second law of The Echo: Repetition creates belief.

FROM BELIEF TO MARKET DOMINANCE

Apple's 2001 introduction of the iPod did not represent the first MP3 player available. Technologically, it was not the greatest. But it didn't matter.

Four years of "Think Different" had conditioned the market to believe that Apple = innovation. This perception wasn't just a nice marketing victory it translated directly into market dominance.

Within three years, iPod owned 70% of the MP3 player market despite being more expensive than competitors and, in many ways, more restrictive (it only worked with iTunes).

This pattern repeated with the iPhone in 2007 and the iPad in 2010. Neither was the first of its kind. Neither had the most advanced specifications. Yet both dominated their categories within months of launch.

Why? Because The Echo had already done the heavy lifting. The market had been conditioned to believe that Apple's products were revolutionary, so they perceived them as revolutionary regardless of specifications or feature comparisons.

When your brand has achieved Echo status, consumers filter reality through the lens you've created. Technical specs and feature comparisons become secondary to the emotional reality your Echo has established.

This is the third law of The Echo: Perception dictates behaviour

CREATING YOUR OWN ECHO: THE THREE ELEMENTS

While few companies will ever achieve Apple's level of market dominance, any brand can apply the principles of The Echo to create greater market influence. The formula requires three elements:

1. Core Truth Amplification

The Echo begins with a kernel of truth that resonates with your target audience. Apple really was founded by visionaries. Apple really did approach technology differently than IBM or Microsoft.

The Echo doesn't create something from nothing it amplifies what already exists.

Your brand's Echo must start with identifying your authentic differentiator, then amplifying it beyond its natural proportion.

Volvo amplified their commitment to car safety until "Volvo" stood for "safety" in the consumer's mind; they did not invent car safety.

Red Bull did not invent energy drinks; instead, they amplified their association with extreme sports until Red Bull stood for pushing limits.

Ask yourself: What authentic truth about our brand could become our dominant market identity if amplified consistently?

2. Message Compression

The human mind doesn't remember paragraphs. It remembers phrases.

"Think Different"

Just Do It; The Ultimate Driving Machine

The Echo asks you to reduce your fundamental truth into a message so strong and brief that it can be repeated repeatedly without losing impact.

This compressed message becomes a mental anchor a cognitive shortcut that carries the full weight of your brand's meaning.

Emphasizing "accelerating the world's transition to sustainable energy," Tesla developed from a small luxury car maker into the front face of future transportation.

Ask yourself: What two-to-five-word phrase best captures the primary difference of our brand?

3. Omnichannel Consistency

The Echo's most important component is consistency across every conceivable touchpoint. This goes beyond merely repeating a phrase; every expression of your brand should confirm the same impression.

When Apple launched "Think Different," this consistency extended to:

- Product design (simplicity, elegance)
- Packaging (minimalist, premium)
- Store experiences (open, interactive)
- Website (clean, intuitive)
- Customer service (knowledgeable, empowered)

Even their famous "1984" Super Bowl commercial, created years earlier, had laid groundwork for the identity of Apple as the rebel against conformity.

The power of The Echo comes not just from saying the same thing repeatedly, but from creating a complete ecosystem where every experience reinforces the same perception.

Ask yourself: How can we ensure every customer touchpoint from marketing to product to service amplifies our core truth?

THE ECHO EFFECT IN ACTION: CASE STUDIES BEYOND APPLE

While Apple provides the quintessential example of The

Echo, countless other brands have deployed this strategy to dominate their markets:

Coca Cola: Happiness in a Bottle

Over a century Coca Cola has connected their beverage with celebration, camaraderie, and pleasure. The formula never changes:

- Core Truth Amplification: Coca-Cola does create moments of simple pleasure
- Message Compression: "Open Happiness"
- Omnichannel Consistency: From Santa Claus imagery to polar bears to the "share a Coke" campaign

The result? Coca-Cola is consumed more than 1.9 billion times per day worldwide despite being essentially flavoured sugar water a triumph of perception over product reality.

Nike: The Champion Within

Nike transformed from a running shoe company to a global symbol of athletic achievement through The Echo:

- Core Truth Amplification: Nike's founders were actually coaches and athletes
- Message Compression: "Just Do It"
- Omnichannel Consistency: From celebrity endorsements to store experiences to product design

The result? Nike commands premium pricing and 62% of the

athletic footwear market in the US because they don't sell shoes they sell achievement.

Tesla: The Future on Wheels

Perhaps the most impressive recent example of The Echo comes from Tesla:

- **Core Truth Amplification:** Tesla's vehicles really are innovative and electric
- **Message Compression:** "Accelerating the world's transition to sustainable energy"
- **Omnichannel Consistency:** From minimalist showrooms to software updates to Elon Musk's persona

The result? Tesla commands 65% of the EV market in the US despite increased competition, and its market capitalization has at times exceeded all other automakers combined.

THE DARK SIDE OF THE ECHO

The psychological power of The Echo carries ethical implications every marketer must consider.

When you understand that repetition creates belief potentially overriding rational analysis you must ensure what you're repeating is truthful and beneficial.

Tobacco companies understood The Echo when they repeatedly associated their products with sophistication, freedom, and masculinity. Political propagandists leverage

The Echo when they repeat simplistic narratives until they're accepted as truth regardless of factual accuracy.

The line between persuasion and manipulation lies in the authenticity of your core truth. Are you amplifying something genuine, or manufacturing a false perception?

This is why the first element Core Truth Amplification is so important. Your Echo must be built on something real, or it will eventually collapse.

CREATING BRAND STICKINESS THROUGH COGNITIVE DESIGN

Beyond the three elements, creating an unshakable brand requires understanding how memory formation works in the human brain. By designing your Echo strategy around the biological mechanisms of memory, you can create brand associations that resist competitive messaging and market changes.

Our brains create stronger neural pathways when information is:

1. Emotionally charged: Apple connected their brand to inspiration and creativity, emotions that create stronger memories than product features. Neuroscience research shows that emotional memories are processed through the amygdala, creating stronger, more persistent imprints than non-emotional information. This explains why we might forget product specifications but remember how a brand made us feel.

2. Pattern disrupting: The "1984" ad and "Think Different" campaign consciously subverted traditional marketing trends, making them more memorable. Our brains are prediction machines and are always expecting the next thing. When a pattern is broken, the brain gets more alert and encodes more intensely. That's why the initial time you drive a new route demands your complete attention, but the tenth time you take it, you hardly register the ride.

3. Identity forming: The most powerful Echoes connect to how people see themselves or who they aspire to be. When brand messaging aligns with personal or aspirational identity, it receives preferential processing in the brain. Research in social psychology shows that identity-relevant information is processed more deeply and remembered more accurately than identity-neutral information.

4. Consistently reinforced: Memory formation requires repetition across time and contexts. The brain strengthens neural connections through a process called long-term potentiation, which requires both repetition and contextual variation. This explains why seeing a brand message across different media (social, print, video) creates stronger memory imprints than seeing it repeatedly in the same context.

5. Distinctively encoded: Messages that stand out through unique visual, verbal, or conceptual elements create stronger memory traces. This is why jingles, distinctive visual assets, and unique brand voices persist in memory they create multiple retrieval pathways in the brain.

When your brand messaging incorporates these elements, it doesn't just communicate it rewires neural pathways, creating what neuroscientists call "potentiation" (the strengthening of neural connections). This biological process transforms fleeting exposure into permanent associations.

This is why people who grew up with Apple's "Think Different" campaign still associate the company with innovation even when competitors may offer more truly innovative features. The neural pathways are so strengthened that contrary evidence is filtered out. The perception has become, for all practical purposes, reality.

THE ECHO IMPLEMENTATION FRAMEWORK

To implement The Echo for your own brand, follow this strategic framework:

Step 1: Truth Mining

Identify 3-5 authentic differentiators about your brand. These must be genuinely true, not aspirational. The most powerful Echoes amplify existing truths rather than manufacturing fictional attributes.

- What was the original vision that inspired your company's founding?
- What do your most loyal customers consistently praise?
- What aspect of your product/service consistently outperforms competitors?

- What origin story elements contain emotional power?
- What values has your organization consistently demonstrated?

From these truths, identify which one has the most potential to become your dominant market identity. The ideal truth has three characteristics: it's authentic to your brand, emotionally resonant with customers, and competitively distinctive in your category.

Consider how REI amplified their co-op structure into the powerful "REI Co-op" Echo that positioned them as fundamentally different from other outdoor retailers, or how Southwest Airlines amplified their operational efficiency into the "Freedom to Fly" Echo that transformed a cost advantage into an emotional benefit.

Step 2: Message Distillation

Work to compress your core truth into its most potent form. The most powerful Echoes are cognitive concentrates ideas so densely packed that they expand in the consumer's mind upon reception.

- Can you express it in 2-5 words?
- Does it evoke emotion?
- Is it distinctive from competitor messaging?
- Does it connect to identity, not just utility?
- Is it flexible enough to evolve with your brand?
- Does it contain implicit competitive contrast?

Test variations of this compressed message with your target audience until you find the formulation that creates the strongest recall and emotional response. Remember that emotional response is more important than rational evaluation customers won't remember what you said, but how you made them feel.

Lululemon distilled their truth into "Yoga-inspired athletic apparel"a phrase that created clear category differentiation while implying a deeper philosophical approach to athletic wear. This wasn't just technical clothing; it was mindful apparel with meaning.

Step 3: Consistency Planning

Audit every customer touchpoint to ensure each reinforces your core truth. The Echo gains power not just from repetition, but from consistency across contexts creating the sense that the message is coming from everywhere.

- Marketing: Does all advertising reinforce the same perception?
- Product: Does the product experience itself deliver on the core truth?
- Service: Do all customer interactions reinforce the perception?
    - Culture: Do employees embody the core truth in their work?
    - Digital: Do your website, app, and online presence reflect the core truth?
    - Physical: Do your physical locations embody your Echo?

  - Partnerships: Do your strategic alliances strengthen your Echo?

Create a "consistency scorecard" to regularly evaluate how well each touchpoint aligns with your Echo. The goal is not perfection at each touchpoint, but cumulative consistency that creates the sense that your Echo is a fundamental truth rather than a marketing message.

Step 4: Repetition Strategy

Develop a multi-year plan for consistent message deployment. The Echo is not a campaign; it's a commitment. Its power accumulates over time, requiring patience and discipline.

- How will you maintain message consistency even when market pressures tempt you to change course?
- What guardrails will you establish to prevent off-message communications?
- How will you evolve the expression of your message without changing its essence?
- What metrics will you use to track Echo penetration in your market?
- How will you resist chasing short-term trends at the expense of long-term Echo formation?
- What governance structure will ensure Echo consistency across departments and years?

The most common mistake brands make is abandoning their Echo before it has time to fully penetrate the market's consciousness. Netflix maintained "DVD by mail" as their

Echo for years before evolving to "Watch Instantly" understanding that premature evolution dilutes Echo power.

THE FUTURE OF YOUR ECHO

As we'll explore in subsequent chapters, creating The Echo is just the beginning. Once established, your brand Echo becomes a strategic asset that can be leveraged for:

- Premium pricing
    - Customer loyalty
    - Market leadership
    - Expansion into adjacent categories
    - Resistance to competitive threats
    - Recovery from setbacks

When Apple faced the 2010 "Antenna gate" controversy with the iPhone 4, their established Echo of innovation and quality allowed them to weather the storm with minimal market impact. The perception they had built was stronger than the temporary reality of a flawed product.

That's the ultimate power of The Echo it creates a perception so strong it can withstand contrary evidence. It's why Harley-Davidson owners tattoo the logo on their bodies. It's why people camp overnight for new Apple products. It's why certain brands become not just preferred, but part of their customers' identities.

THE ECHO IN ACTION: BEYOND TECHNOLOGY

While Apple provides the quintessential example of The Echo, this strategy works across every industry, not just technology.

Consider how LEGO transformed from a struggling toy manufacturer in 2003 to the world's most powerful brand by 2015. Their Echo" Creativity through play" was compressed into the slogan "Play On" and later "Play Well" (the literal meaning of "LEGO" in Danish). This Echo guided every decision, from product development to theme parks to movies.

Or examine how Patagonia created an unshakable position in outdoor apparel with their Echo "We're in business to save our home planet." This wasn't just a CSR statement but a central operating principle that informed everything from their famous "Don't Buy This Jacket" campaign to their materials sourcing to their political activism.

Even commodity industries can deploy The Echo. Morton Salt has maintained market leadership for over a century with the simple Echo "When it rains, it pours," compressed into the iconic image of the girl with the umbrella. This transformed an undifferentiated product (salt) into a trusted staple of American kitchens.

CONCLUSION: BEGIN YOUR ECHO

As we conclude this chapter, remember that The Echo isn't just a marketing strategy it's a fundamental shift in how you approach your relationship with the market.

Most companies behave as if they're in a daily battle for attention, constantly changing tactics and messages in response to market conditions. They communicate like someone shouting different phrases into a canyon, hearing nothing back.

Brands that achieve unshakable market positions understand they're not shouting into a canyon they're programming the canyon itself. Through consistent, strategic repetition of a compressed truth, they change how the market processes information about their category.

Apple didn't just shout "Think Different" into the market. They reprogrammed the market to echo back "innovative" every time someone encountered their brand. The genius of The Echo is that eventually, the market does your marketing for you.

When I work with clients to implement The Echo strategy, I often encounter scepticism: "But we need to respond to market conditions." "Our industry changes too fast." "We need fresh messaging to capture attention." These objections reveal a fundamental misunderstanding of how brand perception forms.

It's precisely because markets change that The Echo works. While competitors chase trends, The Echo provides psychological stability. While other messages come and go, The Echo creates cumulative impact. While others shout louder, The Echo resonates deeper.

That's the power of The Echo and it begins with the decision to focus not on what you say today, but on what you'll still be saying a decade from now. It requires the courage to commit to a singular message in a world obsessed with novelty, and the discipline to maintain that message when short-term thinking demands change.

In the next chapter, we'll explore how perception becomes reality in marketing, and how brands like Tesla engineer consent to make themselves the default choice in their categories.

But first, ask yourself: What truth about your brand, if repeated with Apple-like consistency, could transform your market position from shakeable to unshakable?

The answer to that question is where your Echo begins.

2

PERCEPTION IS REALITY — HOW MANUFACTURED CONSENT OPERATES IN MARKETING

Something strange occurred in 2018 in the car world.

Tesla, which made only 245,000 vehicles in that year, was valued higher than General Motors, which made nearly 9 million vehicles. Wall Street, the public, and the media all concurred: Tesla was the future of transportation, and the old-school car manufacturers were dinosaurs on the verge of becoming extinct.

But how? How did a business that built 35 fewer cars than its competitor end up at the top of the market? How did a business that never ever made any annual profit come to be used interchangeably with the future of transport?

The answer is in what we term manufactured consent strategic control of market perception until it is accepted as fact. Tesla didn't have to produce more than GM to own it in terms of market valuation. It only needed to influence people's understanding of how they perceived the future of transportation.

It is not unique to Tesla. It is the same psychological factor under which high-end brands of water can charge 2000% of the cost of tap water, luxury fashion brands can sell t-shirts for hundreds of dollars, and tech companies can reap loyalty at the level of religious-like fanaticism.

Here in this chapter, we will disassemble the process of how market leaders create consent through perception engineering and set out an overview of how your company can be your category's first choice not by being largest, but by appearing to be most important.

WHEN PERCEPTION TAKES PRECEDENCE

Just let's start with a basic but key fact: objective reality really is second to perceived reality when it comes to marketing.

Keep these market realities in mind:

- Blind tastings on a regular basis consistently demonstrate that consumers can't tell the difference between high-end and low-end vodkas, but Grey Goose costs 400% more.
    - Blind tasting tests reveal that the majority of wine connoisseurs won't be able to identify wines, but when the same wine is labelled on a fancy-looking label compared to a plain bottle, a significantly different rating is given.

- Patients are more responsive to brand-name drugs than to chemically identical generics, even if they're informed that they're chemically identical.

These are not accidents they're expressions of an underlying principle: **perceived value creates actual value.**

The greatest brands know this principle isn't a quirk of consumer behaviour it's the basis of market leadership. They not only appreciate the difference between what is and what is perceived, but they deliberately create it.

THE TESLA PLAYBOOK: MASS-MANUFACTURING PERCEPTION

For some idea of what manufactured consent in practice looks like out there, let's take a look at Tesla's playbook:

Step 1: Control of Narrative Through Leadership

Elon Musk didn't found Tesla as producing better cars; he founded the company as "accelerating the world's transition to sustainable energy." This narrative moved Tesla from being a car company to a movement to change the world.

When old-line automakers were discussing incremental fuel economy gain, Musk was discussing colonizing Mars, neural implants, and transforming energy systems. This introduced a perception asymmetry: when competitors were also entering electric vehicles, they appeared to be followers, not as leaders.

First rule of manufactured consent: **Make the story bigger than your product category.**

Step 2: Symbolic Actions Over Mass Production

Tesla got that symbolism beats production numbers when it comes to influencing perception. Everything Tesla announced was designed for maximum symbolic resonance:

- The Roadster showed electric vehicles can be sexy and quick
  - The Gigafactory showed seriousness about ramping up
  - The polarizing design of the Cybertruck created more buzz than all the rivals' truck debuts combined
  - Placing a Tesla in orbit aboard SpaceX's Falcon Heavy created an unforgettable brand imprint

As Ford and GM manufactured millions of forgettable cars, Tesla was making fewer, but more memorable experiences that found cultural resonance.

The second principle of manufactured consent: **Symbolic actions generate more perception value than incremental production.**

Step 3: Tribal Identity Formation

Tesla did not sell vehicles; it built a tribe bound together by values and beliefs regarding the future. Owners of Tesla didn't buy a car; they joined a movement.

This sense of tribal identification was cemented through:

- Musk's Twitter direct communication with customers
    - Owner-limited software features and updates
    - Shared experience and community events
    - A greater mission than mobility

Even those who couldn't afford Teslas felt connected to the mission of the company and rallied around it in the face of criticism. They turned into perception amplifiers, amplifying Tesla's message at no cost.

The third of the manufactured consent principles: **Make customers identity-driven evangelists.**

Step 4: Manufacturing Scarcity

While other traditional automakers invested billions of dollars persuading individuals their surplus inventory was in demand, Tesla did the opposite. Long waiting lists for cars were not production setbacks but proof of enormous demand.

This artificially induced scarcity created a perception feedback loop:

- Scarcity created perceived value
    - Perceived value created further demand
    - Further demand drove prices up
    - Higher prices sustained premium positioning

The fourth manufactured consent principle: **Scarcity creates more perceived value than abundance.**

Step 5: Reality Distortion Through Future Selling

Tesla was a master at what Steve Jobs referred to as the "reality distortion field" the ability to convince others that the unlikely is not only possible but inevitable.

Tesla was having mass production issues on the Model 3, and yet Musk would introduce the Semi, Roadster 2.0, and Cybertruck. Those future items created a picture of constant innovation that overshadowed today's manufacturing issues.

Some called it manipulative; others called it visionary. This much is certain: it worked Tesla's stock spiked on future, not current, production speculation.

The fifth trick of manufactured consent: Peddle the future to divert from the present.

THE NEUROSCIENCE OF MANUFACTURED REALITY

Why perception engineering works, we need to examine how the brain constructs belief and decides.

Neuroscientists have found that our brains do not objectively process information. Rather, we employ mental heuristics to deal with cognitive load. Mental short cuts make us vulnerable to manipulation by perception in the following predictable ways:

The Availability Heuristic

Our minds guesstimate probability and value according to ease of recall for examples. Tesla captured auto coverage of a low-market-share company, so appeared larger than their production levels intimated.

Should buyers think auto innovation or electric vehicles, automatically they think about Tesla due to this imbalance in availability in people's minds self-reinforcing a circle of importance.

We value more highly input from presumed experts. By presenting himself as vision mastermind, Musk conferred his words historically unprecedented power, even where they conflicted with experts in the field.

Apple employed the same process when Steve Jobs rolled out products as "revolutionary" and "magical." The public didn't critically analyse these assertions they believed them due to Jobs' presumed expertise.

The Social Proof Heuristic

We are reliant on others to determine what is right or desirable. If influencers and early adopters have already embraced Tesla, it has produced cascading social proof that the brand is future-focused.

This is the reason why Tesla remains irrelevant on spending in traditional advertising their campaign leveraged natural human behaviour to emulate perceived leaders and early adopters.

The Framing Effect

The way in which information is presented has a powerful effect on how it is received. Tesla always positioned itself against a future of vision, positioning its rivals against a dated past.

When mass-market automakers rolled out electric vehicle plans, Tesla enthusiasts inquired, "Where's the charging infrastructure?" When Tesla experienced production woes, fans replied, "They're changing the way they make things." Same facts, different framing, vastly different perceptions.

Engineering Default Choice Status

Mastering these rules of psychology is only step 1. True power lies in applying them mercilessly to build default choice status for your brand.

Default choice status happens when consumers instinctively default to your brand as their go-to choice first, even when shopping in highly competitive categories. It's the distinction between being an option and being the standard whereby options are measured.

This is how leaders apply this rule:

1. Control of category definition

The first to category a brand will become the category's default. Not because they're first to market, but because they're first to define how the market thinks about the category.

Uber didn't create the category of ride-hailing, but they defined it as "push a button, get a ride" such a precise definition that it's now the de facto standard expectation. Any other competitor is now measured against how well they match Uber's category definition.

In order to become default choice yourself, you need to capture category definition first, ahead of competitors:

- What 3-5 attributes should constitute your category?
    - How do you make those attributes a part of your brand identity that you can't live without?
    - What category name can you make popular that is a bit biased towards your products?

Airbnb never put itself in the "vacation rental" category it invented the "belonging anywhere" category, which competitors couldn't credibly claim.

2. Perception Gaps Exploitation

Every market has a gap between perceived reality and objective reality. Default choice brands not only recognize such gaps they deliberately make them bigger for their own benefits.

Brands of bottled water take advantage of the difference between perception of safety from tap water (objectively high in the developed world) and subjective sense of safety (in question). They don't have to be dishonest; they just need to make existing gaps in perception larger.

How to spot exploitable perception gaps in your category:

- Where do consumers routinely overestimate or underestimate real differences between choices?
    - Which of its attributes cannot consumers judge objectively?
    - What hopes and fears can be linked to your category?

Red Bull is not cheap to make but is sold at premium prices since it takes advantage of the gap between real and perceived enhancement in performance.

3. Ownership of Language Pattern

What we believe is shaped by what we say. Default choice brands don't simply engage in category discussions they set the terms for those discussions.

Apple doesn't sell "smartphones" they sell "iPhones." This trend in language puts competitors in the second position of being "not-iPhones." When a category generic term is competing with your brand name, and your brand name emerges victorious, you've gained language pattern ownership.

How to construct language pattern ownership:

- What are the terms or expressions that you can bring mainstream which low-key favour your product offering?
    - How can your product naming process facilitate category leadership?

    - What metaphors or analogies establish your brand as the point of natural reference?

Kleenex so comprehensively dominated their category's use pattern that consumers employ the company name as the generic one, substituting the phrases "Kleenex" with "facial tissue."

4. Selective Evidence Amplification

Customers never have full information regarding a category. Default choice brands intentionally highlight evidence favouring their superiority and neglects counter-evidence.

Tesla highlights battery range and acceleration and neglects mentioning manufacturing quality. This is not lying this is intentional highlight of positive comparison points.

In order to employ selective evidence amplification:

- What measures or comparison points inherently work in your favour?
    - How do you make these numbers look more important than others?
    - Which review criteria or industry standards need to be redefined?

When Domino's emphasized delivery speed, they moved the pizza category competition axis from "best tasting" (which they lost) to "most convenient" (which they won).

5. Manipulation of Choice Architecture

Default choices don't occur by chance they're the product of well-crafted choice architecture that makes one option feel like the default.

Netflix crafted their user experience such that binge-watching is the path of least resistance. Amazon made one-click shopping the default. These aren't convenience features they're choice architecture nudges that create default behaviour.

How to craft good choice architecture:

- How do you make friction in selecting your brand lower than other alternatives?
    - What order choice naturally results in your solution?
    - How do you position the alternatives as "extra steps" or "unnecessary complexity"?

Apple's platform is the ultimate choice architecture once you own one Apple device, every subsequent buy decision is subtly pushed towards another Apple device.

THE ETHICS OF MANUFACTURED CONSENT

Before we go any further, we must address the ethics of perception engineering.

Building things is potent and power comes with great responsibility. The distinction between persuasion and manipulation lies less in the methods employed, but rather in the underlying reality that they point out or hide.

Some of the following are ethical principles:

1. Amplification of Truth vs. Construction of Fictions: Ethical perception engineering inflates realities and not fictions. Tesla is actually advancing innovation with electric cars; they're just strategically inflating that truth in proportion to other realities.

2. Congruence of Value Delivery: The perception you build must align with the value you deliver. When brands build perceptions that they cannot deliver through experience, things begin to go wrong.

3. Transparency About Technique: You don't need to reveal your perception engineering technique, but customers should be able to verify your base claims if they want to check.

The most effective sustainable manufactured consent techniques operate like magicians who tell you that they will deceive youthe audience consents to being deceived because the experience itself generates actual value.

CASE STUDY: HOW YETI ENGINEERED DEFAULT CHOICE STATUS

To observe those principles at play outside of Tesla, think how YETI took the bland cooler from being a commodity item to a luxury status symbol.

In 2006, coolers were just practical goods that cost between $20 and $50. In 2018, YETI was selling effectively the same product class for $300-$1,300 and had become the go-to standard for outdoors people even at premium price.

Their manufactured consent strategy:

1. Category Redefinition: YETI didn't compete in the "cooler" category they invented the "premium outdoor gear" category, making something so humble aspirational.

2. Tribal Identity Formation: YETI didn't sell coolers they sold membership in the real outdoorsman tribe. Their "Built for the Wild" campaign made you think that purchasing any other cooler somehow made you fake.

3. Selective Evidence Amplification: Instead of competing on price (where they were losing ground), YETI emphasized super-durability tests bear attacks, throw-offs off cliffs and turned the spotlight on the one characteristic where they excelled.

4. Manufactured Scarcity: Limited-release offerings, rationed availability, and high-priced points all conspired to generate a perception of scarcity that intensified desirability.

5. Hyping of the Authority Heuristic: YETI invited the word-of-mouth endorsements of hunting and fishing guides those authoritative persons whose endorsement meant more than universal commercialism.

Result: YETI enthusiasts sport cooler-handles on trucks and boats like a badge. They decal cars with YETI. They leap to the company's defines when other people slander. The cooler's become an identity icon all because of manipulated perception engineering.

USING YOUR PERCEPTION ENGINEERING TOOL

Now that we've identified the principles of manufactured consent, let's set up a step-by-step tool for using this strategy for your brand:

Phase 1: Perception Audit

Start by objectively evaluating how you are perceived currently:

- How do customers perceive your category today?
    - How do they decide?
    - Where is your brand on their perception map today?
    - What are the gaps between perceived reality and actual reality in your category?

This audit creates the gap between current perception and your target perception.

Phase 2: Perception Target Definition

Next, define your target perception clearly:

- What 3-5 traits should you embody in your category?

- Which of these can you own credibly?
- What would be the optimal view of your brand?
- What story would make your brand the default?

Keep in mind, your goal is not to be "best" in someone else's pre-defined system, but to build a new perceptual system where you're the default.

Phase 3: Strategic Perception Levers

Set the specific levers that you will use to shift perception:

Narrative Control: What story will you tell for your category and brand?

Symbolic Actions: What high-visibility actions will demonstrate your story?

Tribal Markers: How will customers mark themselves as members of your brand tribe?

Language Patterns: What words or phrases will you claim and make mainstream?

Perception Gaps: Which perception-reality gaps will you take advantage of?

For each lever, create specific tactics and measurement metrics.

Phase 4: Consent Manufacturing Campaign

Finally, carry out your plan with a coordinated campaign:

Consistent Messaging: Make every communication support your target perception

Experience Alignment: Provide experiences which confirm your built perception

Feedback Amplification: Find and share customer feedback that confirms your account

Opposition Framing: Frame opponents in terms that makes your response the natural option

Persistence Planning: Create a multi-year commitment to perception engineering

The biggest trap is underestimating the timeframe for manufactured consent to become ingrained. Tesla's reputation for being the future car did not take years but rather happened over years.

MEASURING MANUFACTURED CONSENT

How can you know whether your perception engineering is successful? Look for these signs:

1. Price Elasticity Increases: As manufactured consent takes hold, price sensitivity decreases. Tesla buyers barely ever price shop.

2. Media Framing Shifts: Journalists begin using your language and framing when they mention the category.

3. Comparison Asymmetry Emerges: Competitors are compared to you, not vice versa, increasingly.

4. Identity-Based defence Appears: Customers begin defending your brand spontaneously.

5. Category Definition Control: Your brand is the reference point for category expectations.

When these signals occur, you're no longer just a choice in your space; you're becoming the default choice.

CONCLUSION: FROM PERCEPTION TO REALITY

With that in mind, as we wrap up this chapter, keep in mind that perception engineering is not about the creation of illusions; it's about carefully amplifying facts to establish new market realities.

Tesla gained its position as the most valuable automaker without being deceitful. They knew with rich information but limited attention that perceived relevance creates real relevance.

Your own brand can use these same disciplines on whatever scale. You don't require Elon Musk's number of Twitter followers or Apple's advertising budget to start building consent within your category. You just need to know that in markets, perception is reality; and perception can be engineered.

In the following chapter, we will discover how this manufactured consent generates "The Illusion of Choice"; the psychological process by which customers think they are making free will decisions when, in reality, they are being steered down well-laid-out paths.

But first, ask yourself: If your brand could control how customers think about your whole category, what would that thought be? The answer is the first step toward making your brand the default choice.

3

THE ILLUSION OF CHOICE — WHY CUSTOMERS BUY WHAT

They're Told

"I drink Coke, not Pepsi."

"I'm a Mac person, not a PC person."

"I drive German cars, not Japanese cars."

We all make these sorts of claims. We use them as badges of identity, assuming that they're statements of real personal preference built on reason. We assume that we picked these brands because they're better, because they're in our values, because they're the real us.

What if this sense of choice is really illusion and not reality?

Suppose that our strongest preferences; our brand loyalties that we most loudly advocate, are really not the result of our own independent reasoning but of highly skilled psychological forces designed to make choice an illusion and circumvent the risk of decision?

Here we will discuss the biggest paradox in consumer psychology: the more customers feel they have made an independent decision, the better they have been directed toward a predetermined solution.

THE PEPSI PARADOX: WHEN TASTE ISN'T IMPORTANT

Pepsi introduced in 1975 the longest-running ad ever conceived: The Pepsi Challenge. Unlabelled glasses of Coke and Pepsi were sent to America's mall consumers, then they were instructed to say what they preferred best. The result was miraculous, more chose Pepsi in blind taste tests."

Pepsi executives were thrilled. Now, they had scientific proof that Pepsi tasted better than Coca-Cola. Equipped with that information, they unveiled a fiercely worded campaign highlighting those statistics, hoping market share would follow taste preference.

It didn't.

Despite irrefutable proof that customers enjoyed Pepsi blind taste, Coca-Cola dominated the market. Even more fascinating, when identical taste tests were conducted with brands specified, preferences flipped; the very same people who enjoyed Pepsi blind preferred Coke once they were told what they were drinking.

This became known as "The Pepsi Paradox" afterward, and what it indicates is a simple reality about consumer culture: Cogent product attributes (i.e., taste) are apt to be overcome by brand reputation in terms of consumer preference.

Why?

In 2004, neuroscientist Read Montague attempted to do this with brain scanning technology involving fMRI. His study, in the journal Neuron, described a somewhat surprising result. When individuals drank unlabelled soda, the brain's reward system (the ventral putamen) was activated based on taste preference. But when they believed they were drinking Coca-Cola, other parts of the brain involved in memory, emotion, and self-referential thinking were also activated.

What Montague discovered is that consumers weren't consuming a product, they were consuming identity, a meaning construct, one that was evolving over time. When they consumed Coca-Cola, they weren't selecting by taste; they were affirming narrative to self already established.

That's the first principle of the Illusion of Choice: **People don't choose products; people choose confirmations of self.**

BEYOND DRINKS: THE FALSE ILLUSION OF CHOICE IN EVERY CATEGORY

The Pepsi Paradox is not exclusive to colas. The same applies to almost all consumer products:

- People cannot reliably distinguish between cheap and expensive vodkas in blind tests, but Grey Goose and Belvedere enable price premiums of 400% or more.

- People who like wine repeatedly cannot discriminate between wines when tested blind, and preferentially rate the same wine differently depending on bottles which have different labels.
    - Luxury car owners say that the car drives better, but when brand recognition is stripped away under controlled conditions, they often can't tell luxury from mass-market cars.

Owners of iPhone argue that their device is more intuitive, yet research suggests that usage of features one does not know about in iOS and Android has a virtually similar learning curve.

Either way, objective reality of the product is worth less than subjective reality of the brand. It's not that shoppers are insane – it's merely that brands have gotten away with creating the fiction of objective choice identity claims.

THE NEUROSCIENCE OF NON-CHOICE

To understand how illusion of choice plays out, we must look at how the brain really makes decisions.

The model of the rational consumer choice tells us to weigh our choices, weigh the benefits and losses, and make the better selection. We're drawn to it because it is the way that we want to view ourselves as reasonable people and rational decision makers.

But neuroscience reveals to us a different world. The brain processes the overwhelming majority of information automatically, trusting to an underlying system of heuristics and mental shortcuts in order to conserve on cognitive load. Instead of creating new judgments for every decision, we call upon current mental templates that facilitate decision-making.

Decision scientist and Nobel prize winner Daniel Kahneman describes it as "System 1" thinking; rapid, automatic, and intuitive. The opposite of this is "System 2" thinking; slow, rule-based, and effortful.

This is a psychological component that one needs to remember as customer decisions are guided more than 95% by System 1.

This is to note that although they inform researchers that they decide (e.g., "I compared features carefully," "I did my research"), most consumer buying decisions derive from rapid unconscious processing based on pre-existing mental models.

The best brands do not simply inform consumers what to think about products; they establish the mental models upon which all evaluation takes place.

IDENTITY-BASED CHOICE ARCHITECTURE

So how do brands build these mental frameworks? By means of the application of what I call "Identity-Based Choice Architecture"; deliberate design of choice pathways that nudge consumers to predetermined conclusions as free choice is the illusion created.

This model has four components:

1. Identity Anchoring

The strongest method to push a consumer's decision is to make it feel like an extension of who they already believe they are. That is why brands do so much work to match up with identity-creating signifiers:

- Harley-Davidson does not sell motorcycles; it sells rebellion and freedom
    - Patagonia does not sell climbing gear; it sells greenery
    - Apple does not sell technology; it sells thinking differently
    - Jeep does not sell SUVs; it sells adventure and capability

By positioning themselves on present identity factors, these brands transform the choice of a product into an act of identification instead of an exercise of judgment. Their choice becomes one of saying "This is who I am."

2. Contrast Framing

Once identity anchoring is established, brands construct cognitive schemes that frame competitive relationships in a way favourable to their own standing. This involves defining the criterion used to evaluate alternatives.

Consider the ways different automobile brands frame the category:

- BMW: "The Ultimate Driving Machine" (defining driving ability as the primary criterion)
- Volvo: "For Life" (defining safety as the primary criterion)
- Lexus: "The Pursuit of Perfection" (positioning refinement as the key issue)

These are not advertising slogans; they are competitive constructs that make quality judgments. Use BMW's construct, and you will judge all cars first on drive dynamics; BMW's biggest strength. Use Volvo's construct, and safety is the key issue; Volvo's reputation heritage.

The strength of contrast framing is that it operates below the level of conscious awareness. Individuals don't even realize they've taken on a particular evaluative template; they simply sense that they're rendering an objective judgment on "what matters."

3. Choice Reduction

While appearing to offer choice, sophisticated marketers eliminate meaningful decision-making to the extent that consideration is restricted. This is achieved through using what psychologists call "consideration set management"; manipulating what decisions the purchaser will seriously consider.

Proof shows that consumers fail to register 2-3 choices in a present category even when there are many more. Such brands already won half the battle.

Consideration set dominance discovers brands through:

- Perceptual Familiarity: Familiarity is sufficient to produce a bias (the mere exposure effect)
    - Mental Availability: Theoretically freely available when a category need arises
    - Distinct Assets: Having visual or vocal signatures leading to immediate recognition
    - Category Association: Being in the mind related to the product category itself

Coca-Cola doesn't need to demonstrate that it's better than 500 colas; it only needs to get consumers to think "cola" and say, "Pepsi or Coke"; ideally "Coke, or perhaps Pepsi."

4. Post-Purchase Reinforcement

The last element of choice architecture is post-purchase. The trailblazing brands craft experiences that validate the purchase decision, affirming the narrative that not only did they make the best choice, but that they made the only sensible one.

Apple's packaging excellence, Zappos' customer service, Disney's fastidiousness; these aren't nice perks; they're caring additions to the decision-making process. They're saying, "You made a good choice," and confirming the psychological template for the next time.

Confirmation post-purchase is extremely valuable because of another psychological principle: cognitive dissonance. Having previously reached a brand decision, consumers begin to filter information in a way to reinforce their decision. Brands that make it easy to find reams of confirmation material facilitate the natural process.

ENGINEERING THE ILLUSION: THE COCA-COLA PLAYBOOK

To see Identity-Based Choice Architecture in action, let's examine how Coca-Cola has remained market leader despite the Pepsi Paradox:

Step 1: Identity Anchoring

Coca-Cola has aligned itself with timeless American values and experiences since the 1930s:

- Family togetherness (holiday-themed advertising)
  - Patriotism (patriotic support behind troops, Olympic involvement)
  - Real happiness (plenty of "happiness" messaging)
  - Tradition and nostalgia (consistent visual brand)

These are not mushy emotions; they're identity cues that put Coca-Cola inside Americans' concept of self. Losing them is, subconsciously, losing those parts of American identity.

Step 2: Contrast Framing

Coca-Cola's stroke of genius was to put the cola category in the context of "the real thing"; to make authenticity, rather than taste, the reference point that decides. Their enduring "It's the real thing" campaign was a slogan, but a substitute frame that defined Pepsi as "the imitator" in taste, or in some other way.

This positioning was so strong that when, in 1985, Coca-Cola launched "New Coke" (which actually fared better on taste tests), customers complained. They were not rejecting a taste; they were rejecting a breach of the authenticity paradigm that Coca-Cola had created.

Step 3: Choice Reduction

Coca-Cola achieves consideration set dominance by:

- Ubiquitous distribution (being everywhere)
  - Distinctive assets (the contour bottle, red, dynamic ribbon)
  - Culture pervasiveness (sponsorships, product placements, extent of advertising)

These behaviours have the effect of such that upon hearing "cola," one thinks Coca-Cola immediately. Choice is now "Coke or not; Coke," not peer choice.

Step 4: Post-Purchase Reinforcement

Choice is reinforced by:

- Experience consistency (the product never variant)
  - Cultural sanction (showing Coke being consumed in desired locations)

    - Belongness (Coke sharing adverts, social media presence)

These variables form a persistent cycle of preference for decision reaffirming mental design in anticipation of future determinations.

APPLYING IDENTITY-BASED CHOICE ARCHITECTURE TO YOUR BUSINESS

But then how do you apply these to make your business seem like it provides choice? Apply the strategic process outlined here:

Step 1: Mapping Identity

Begin by decide on those identity variables most related to your business and industry:

- What identity markers lie beneath your target consumers already?
    - Which of those are likely to actually be associated with your brand's heritage or personality?
    - What identity aspirations are present among your target customers?
    - How can your brand facilitate identity expression or extension?

The strongest identity connections aren't created; they're discovered. Look for existing identity elements that naturally align with your brand's inherent strengths or story.

YETI coolers learned that outdoor authenticity was a strong identity marker for their target consumer segment; even among customers who rarely ever engaged in hard-core outdoor activities. By leveraging this identity factor, they made a functional product an identity statement.

Phase 2: Frame Building

Next build the evaluative framework that serves your brand:

- What norms would be second nature to virtues of your brand?
    - How do you apply those criteria to get to your values-to-features move?
    - How do you say it in a way that makes the criteria the "clear" way to measure the category?
    - How do you make your competitor's strengths be a secondary consideration, diplomatically?

As I mentioned before, the goal is not to play the game better; it is to alter the game. Be not better at the game, but alter the game.

Enterprise Rent-A-Car altered the basis of comparison from "lowest price" (where they'd lose) to "we'll pick you up"; setting convenience, not price, as the category's basis of differentiation.

Phase 3: Consideration Set Dominance

Plan to put your brand in the skinny consideration set:

- What are distinctive brand assets that you can buy and engage?
    - How do you create mental availability at category point-of-entry positions?
    - What kind of purchase cue can you craft?
    - How do you create mental shortcuts to your brand?

The battle for consideration takes place before the process of conscious decision-making. First-to-mind brands enjoy an enormous head start.

Phase 4: Decision Validation System

Establish systematic ways to validate the customer's decision:

- How does your first use or unboxing experience affirm the smartness of choosing your brand?
    - What post-purchase communications affirm the brand narrative?
    - How do customers become evangelists that confirm others' choices?
    - What sense of belonging or community can you create for your brand?

The point of purchase is the moment when the customer is most attuned to proof confirming or denying their choice. Offering plenty of corroboration leads to brand champions and loyal customers.

THE ETHICS OF CHOICE ENGINEERING

As we go along, we must engage in the ethics of what we do here. The design of the illusion of choice is a heavy responsibility.

The following approaches are psychologically robust. They operate below the level of conscious awareness and can overrule objective judgment. Such power entails ethical application:

1. **Reality-Based Identity Anchoring:** Whatever identity bonds you establish will need to anchor in tough realities about the brand, not in made-up content. Customers will ultimately call out made-up claims of identity.

2. **Value-Augmenting Framing**: Your evaluation model must reveal objectively salient traits and not deceive consumers over importance.

3. **Fair Consideration Set Competition**: Coming out on top in the consideration set must depend on excellent brand development, rather than underhand tactics to sabotage deserving competitors.

4. **Honest Validation:** Post-consumption verification must validate a genuinely good choice and not mask shortcomings with your product or service.

The difference between manipulation and persuasion is whether your choice architecture leads consumers to make decisions that ultimately serve them. The most sustainable choice architectures connect success at the brand level to customer value.

CASE STUDY: IKEA'S MASTERY OF CHOICE ARCHITECTURE

To see these principles applied successfully outside the beverage category, look at how IKEA has built one of the world's greatest choice architectures:

Identity Anchoring

IKEA bases itself on the healthy identity drivers:

- Functional creativity
    - Environmental consciousness
    - Self-sufficiency and capability

These are not brand attributes; they are identity markers for how IKEA's target market views themselves.

Instruction:

IKEA's "Democratic Design" tagline is the standard for furniture dissection:

- Form (aesthetic form)
    - Function (practical functionality)
    - Quality (firm build)
    - Sustainability (green accountability)
    - Affordability (affordable costs)

This positioning positions competitors on one side or another of being less democratic (high-end design firms) or less design; focused (discount furniture retailers). IKEA is precisely in its own self-definition sweet spot.

Choice Reduction

IKEA overwhelms consideration by:

- Emotionally engaging shopping experience (the IKEA experience)
    - Iconic catalogue (world's most read publication)
    - Sentimental naming convention tradition (Scandinavian product names)
    - Distinctively recognizable visual brand (blue and yellow, flat-pack boxes)

These factors make IKEA the first word that springs to mind when people consider furniture, particularly for their target segments.

Decision Validation

IKEA supports customers' choices by:

- Success of assembly (proud feeling of having done it yourself)
    - Social validation (all around customers have it in their houses)
    - Relationship continuation (food, service, IKEA Family)
    - Price transparency (promptly visible price labels on all demonstration pieces)

The end result is a decision architecture so carefully crafted that customers believe they have made an informed selection of IKEA by rational analysis, while IKEA has intentionally constructed the thought construct upon which all furniture decisions are made.

THE FUTURE OF CHOICE ARCHITECTURE: DIGITAL ASYMMETRY

In the future, choice architecture is becoming increasingly powerful due to what I have called "digital asymmetry"; the increasingly large gap between what brands know about consumers and what consumers know about brands.

Due to data harvesting, brands now have access to information on:

- Consumer browsing behaviour
    - Past purchasing behaviour
    - Past locations
    - Social networks
    - Content interests
    - Emotional states (sentiment analysis)

This opens hitherto unprecedented scope for personalized choice architecture; individual identity elements, as and when presented.

The leading brands already build adaptive choice architectures that vary based on individual consumers, rather than the perspective of choice, but rather the perspective of customized choice.

Amazon's algorithm-driven recommendations, Netflix suggestions, and Spotify playlist suggestions all operate on the same logic; they nudge choice while generating a perception of discovery and autonomous decision.

CONCLUSION: FROM ILLUSION TO INFLUENCE

This chapter is worth recalling as we conclude it; the illusion of choice isn't deception; it's understanding the dynamics of consumer decision-making.

Consumers don't wish to wade through dozens of objectively comparable options. They don't wish to do extensive feature comparisons or taste testing with each purchase. They wish to make decisions aligned with their self-concept and values, with little mental effort.

The best brands accomplish this. They don't have to compete on consideration against an overpopulated consideration set; they create the mental models to which their entire category is compared. They don't compete for preference by the rules; they create the rules by which victory is certain.

This is why Coca-Cola adores market leadership in spite of the Pepsi Paradox. It's why Apple adores premium prices in spite of having perfect substitutes. It's why some brands are category synonyms and yet others are substitutable choices.

By seeing and experiencing the Identity-Based Choice Architecture, your business accomplishes the same- not by persuading people to choose you over another but by reducing the relevance of choices to who they are.

In the next chapter, we'll explore how to craft your master story- your core story that gives the heart of your choice architecture and positions your brand as an extension of your customers' self.

4

THE CORE STORY — BUILDING YOUR MARKET OWNERSHIP STRATEGY

Nike was in trouble in 1987.

Reebok had surpassed them as the number one athletic shoe company. Their market share had fallen from 50% to 18%. Adidas was picking up speed. Nike, after dominating for years, had become another sportswear company struggling to be heard in an ever more crowded marketplace.

Then something amazing happened.

During an agency meeting with Wieden+Kennedy, the ad team at Nike was debating a new ad campaign. From the tale of Gary Gilmore, a killer who was to be executed and uttered the last words on death row, "Let's do it," copywriter Dan Wieden jotted down on a scrap of paper, "Just Do It."

With those three words, Nike didn't release an ad campaign. They established a foundational narrative that would turn them from a shoe brand into a worldwide movement. A story so potent that it not only sold goods- it altered the way that millions of individuals conceived of themselves, their possibilities, and their connection with success.

"Just Do It" wasn't about shoes. It was about human potential. It was about overcoming internal resistance. It was about the universal struggle between action and hesitation.

By 2022, Nike's revenue would exceed $46 billion- nearly 10 times their revenue when "Just Do It" launched. More significantly, they would transform from a product-focused company into something far more valuable: the owner of achievement as a concept in the consumer's mind.

This is the strength of what I refer to as the Core Narrative- the master story that determines not only what your brand delivers, but what it signifies in the marketplace and the culture. When done right, a Core Narrative does not simply place your product; it achieves total market ownership of an idea, an emotion, or a human requirement.

In this chapter, we'll crack the code on how companies such as Nike create these market-leading stories and give you a framework for creating your own Core Narrative strategy that gets customers emotionally attached to your success.

FROM PRODUCT STORY TO MARKET OWNERSHIP

Most brands share product stories. Great brands share market ownership stories.

The distinction is important:

- A product story tells you why your product is better

- A market ownership narrative accounts for why your category can't be divorced from your brand

Have a look at these examples:

Product Story: "Our running shoes are cushioned and have more responsive materials."

Market Ownership Story: "Just Do It"- owning athletic achievement itself.

Product Story: "Our search engine offers more relevant results."

Market Ownership Story: "Google it"- owning information discovery.

Product Story: "Our coffee shops provide premium drinks in a welcoming setting."

Market Ownership Story: "The Third Place"- owning the space between work and home.

The greatest brands aren't competing in markets; they're defining markets. Their Core Narratives build perceptual monopolies where rivals might occupy physical space but not psychological space.

THE ANATOMY OF A MARKET-OWNING CORE NARRATIVE

An extremely effective Core Narrative consists of five building blocks:

1. The Universal Truth

At the heart of every market-dominating story is a universal human truth- a comment about human nature, desire, fear, or aspiration that appeals across demographics and cultures.

Nike's universal truth: Everyone encounters internal resistance when striving for achievement.

Apple's universal truth: Creative individuals want tools that eliminate barriers to expression.

Disney's universal truth: People of every age yearn for magical experiences beyond the routine of daily life.

Your universal truth should be:

- Emotionally compelling (appealing to fundamental human needs)
- Widespread (applicable to your entire target audience)
- Timeless (not subject to today's fads)
- Immediately identifiable (needing no explanation)

The power of a universal truth is that it's self-evident. When others encounter it, they don't need to be convinced; they just recognize something they've always known but never expressed.

2. The Market Connection

Universal truth by itself isn't sufficient. Your Core Narrative needs to establish a plausible, unique link between this truth and your brand's category or product.

Nike linked achievement to athletic gear and apparel.

Apple attached creative expression to technology.

Disney attached magical experiences to entertainment.

This attachment must come across as:

- Natural (not contrived or forced)
- Exclusive (hard for the competition to emulate)
- Value-adding (increase the relevance of your category)
- Ownable (consistent with your true capabilities)

The market attachment turns intangible human requirements into concrete market opportunities where your brand is best suited to deliver.

3. The Proprietary Point of View

Every strong Core Story has a unique perspective that sets apart the way your brand speaks to the universal truth.

Nike's take: Greatness is achieved through doing, not planning or being perfect.

Apple's take: Great design is about simplicity, not complexity.

Patagonia's take: Business can be a force for environmental good, not merely profit.

Your own proprietary point of view should:

- Subvert category norms
- Show your true values and heritage
- Establish natural competitive contrast
- Provide a new perspective on well-known challenges

This view becomes the lens by which consumers consider all possibilities in your category, giving your method a built-in benefit.

4. The Narrative Activation

A Core Narrative is not a positioning statement, but rather an engaging tale that solicits participation. It needs to provide definable roles for your brand and for your customers.

Nike enacts their narrative by casting:

- Consumers as potential heroes facing resistance
    - Nike products as enablers of breakthrough action
    - Nike as the wise mentor encouraging decisive movement

This activation framework creates:

- Clear customer identity ("I am someone who pushes through limitations")
- Clear brand identity ("We are the catalyst for achievement")

- Clear relationship dynamic ("We believe in your potential and equip your journey")

Effective narrative activation turns passive customers into heroes in a living story in which your brand serves as a supporting actor.

5. The Cultural Tension

And finally, the strongest Core Narratives draw upon cultural tensions; the differences between how things are and how they ought to be or could be.

Nike exploited the tension between mundane performance and remarkable potential.

Apple capitalized on tension between human creativity and technological complexity.

Dove capitalized on tension between authentic self-acceptance and beauty industry standards.

Your cultural tension should:

- Be urgent and unresolved
- Resonate with larger social discourse
- Imply that your brand has the solution
- Build organic emotional investment

By placing your brand in these tensions, you're raising its stature from commercial product to cultural voice calling for substantive change.

BUILDING YOUR CORE STORY: THE STRATEGIC BLUEPRINT

With an understanding of the anatomy of an owning narrative, let's look at how you can build one for your brand:

Step 1: Truth Dredging

Start with defining the universal human truths for your category:

- What deep human needs, desires, or problems does your category solve?
- What emotional states come before, are during, or come after interaction with your category?
- What timeless human experiences connect to your offering?
- What unspoken aspirations or fears drive decisions in your category?

The most compelling truths tend to be hiding in plain sight-they're so basic that category participants are taking them for granted.

Method: Interview customers through "aspiration interviews," not asking about your products but about their greater goals and pain points. Listen for common themes that cut across individual features or benefits.

Step 2: Opportunity Mapping

Then, look at how your brand can genuinely assert a proprietary relationship to these truths:

- What elements of your brand history relate to recognized truths?
- What abilities or assets allow you to speak to these truths uniquely?
- What founder story aspects indicate genuine connection to these truths?
- What brand behaviors indicate allegiance to these truths?

Your connection needs to be believable and defendable- backed by real brand attributes, not marketing assertions.

Method: Develop a "truth-to-capability matrix" charting discovered truths against your true strengths, seeking the best natural fit.

Step 3: Perspective Development

Next, define your unique perspective on the truth-opportunity relationship:

- In what ways does your strategy break from traditional category wisdom?
- What new insights has your brand gained regarding tackling the underlying truth?
- What philosophical position characterizes your category approach?
- What category assumptions about your category would you uphold even if they were not popular?

Your point of view should generate natural tension with rivals without calling them out directly.

Method: Perform a "conventional wisdom audit" by enumerating all typical category presumptions, then determining which ones your brand might plausibly contradict.

Step 4: Activation Architecture

Construct the blueprint to bring your story to life:

- What is the role your customer plays in the story?
- What is the role of your brand to the customer?
- What change does your story deliver?
- What barriers does your story overcome?

This structure generates the template for coherent narrative presentation across touchpoints.

Process: Develop a "narrative journey map" illustrating the emotional and functional evolution customers go through when interacting with your Core Narrative.

Step 5: Cultural Resonance

Finally, align your story with wider cultural trends and tensions:

- What social conversations align with your narrative?
- What cultural shifts support or threaten your narrative?
- What communities would naturally champion your narrative?
- What opposing narratives would your story challenge?

This cultural dimension elevates your narrative from a brand story to a meaningful movement.

Method: Conduct a "cultural tension scan" identifying unresolved contradictions in society that your narrative helps address or resolve.

NARRATIVE COMPRESSION: FROM STRATEGY TO EXPRESSION

Once you have crafted your Core Narrative approach, you need to condense it into statements that can transfer smoothly through culture:

The Narrative Statement

First, write an all-encompassing internal narrative statement that encapsulates all five elements:

"Nike believes that everyone has the potential for athletic success (universal truth), but internal resistance keeps them from acting (cultural tension). Unlike other sports companies that are built upon elite performance, Nike envisions athletic potential in all people (proprietary perspective). By offering both performance gear and inspirational inspiration (market connection), Nike enables individuals to get past hesitation and reach their potential (narrative activation)."

This full statement directs internal decision-making but is too complicated for use outside.

The Narrative Tagline

Then, distil this statement into a catchy tagline that evokes the entire narrative:

"Just Do It"

These three words summarize Nike's whole narrative approach- pointing to the universal reality (action is needed to achieve), projecting the cultural conflict (dilemma vs. action), proposing the proprietorial standpoint (action instead of perfection), hinting at the market linkage (apparatus that facilitates performance), and stimulating the customer role (you are the one who has to do something).

The strongest narrative taglines function as if they were zip files- short enough to be transported efficiently but expanding into whole meaning systems when delivered.

The Narrative System

Lastly, create the detailed system of how your story will be realized:

Visual expressions: How does your story equate to imagery and form?

Verbal expressions: What word patterns capture your story?

Experience expressions: How do customer experiences express your story?

Product expressions: How do offerings themselves embody your story?

Cultural expressions: How does your story intersect with larger social dialogue?

Nike's story architecture ranges from their marketing imagery (ordinary people doing extraordinary things) to product name (deciding on names after athletes) to store experience (set up as if they're training facilities for athletes instead of the usual stores).

Having a completely consistent narrative structure guarantees an assurance that your Core Narrative shapes every element of your brand expression. This will lead to an integral presence in the market that is hard, if not impossible, to replicate by competitors.

Other than Words: Integrating Narrative into Business Strategy

The most influential Core Narratives extend beyond marketing- they shape critical business decisions:

Product Development

Nike's story guided their growth from running shoes to total athletic equipment, apparel, and digital services- all in service of the "Just Do It" philosophy.

Partnership Strategy

Nike's story decided who they sponsored- typically those athletes who represented breakthrough accomplishment over technical achievement.

Innovation Focus

Nike's story focused their R&D dollars on innovations that took barriers away from athletic performance for amateur athletes, not just professionals.

Organizational Culture

Nike's story impacted their internal culture, producing a performance-driven environment that matched their outside message.

When your Core Narrative informs these basic business choices, it builds consistency between what you say and what you do- the starting point of true brand building.

The Courage to Own a Narrative

Creating a genuinely market-owning Core Narrative takes courage. It means:

Claiming territory larger than your current position- Nike didn't wait until they dominated sports to claim achievement; they claimed achievement to dominate sports.

Committing to a perspective despite changing trends- Powerful narratives aren't chased; they're maintained even when market pressures suggest otherwise.

Making some people uncomfortable- The strongest narratives create natural opposition, alienating some to deeply connect with others.

Investing before results are proven- Narrative ownership is established through long-term commitment prior to market results validating its success.

The brands that gain authentic market ownership recognize that their Core Narrative is not merely one aspect of their approach- it's the master organizing principle from which all other choices emanate.

CONCLUSION: FROM STORYTELLING TO STORY-OWNING

As we end this chapter, keep in mind that the distinction between good brands and great brands is not the quality of their storytelling, but the totality of their story-owning.

Nike doesn't merely tell stories of accomplishment; they own accomplishment as an idea in the mind of the consumer. When someone anywhere on the planet thinks about overcoming their limits, "Just Do It" instinctively resonates in their mind.

This is the ultimate aim of your Core Narrative- not to have an entertaining story about your brand, but to have a fundamental human truth so thoroughly possessed that consumers can't consider that truth without considering you.

Later in the book, we will discuss how to amplify your Core Narrative by means of calculated repetition that makes your message unavoidable even with today's fragmented media.

But first, ask yourself: What fundamental human truth can your brand credibly claim? The answer to that question is where your market dominance starts.

5

THE REPETITION FORMULA — MAKING YOUR MESSAGE UNIGNORABLE

Donald Trump repeated the term "Make America Great Again" over 2,000 times in speeches during campaign rallies, in tweets, and in interviews during his presidential bid in 2016. His political adversaries were dismissive of it as simplistic. Critics ridiculed it as empty. The pundits ridiculed it as meaningless words.

But by the day of the election, those four words had sunk so deep into American consciousness that they had transcended a slogan- they had become a cultural movement, acknowledged by fans and foes alike. The words were on millions of red hats, ignited endless arguments, and eventually led to an improbable electoral victory.

It was no coincidence. It was the product of hard message reinforcement- the calculated use of repeated words and pictures with such inarguable consistency that it can't help but be followed.

Political campaigns are aware of this force. Media outlets use it on a daily basis. And the world's most powerful brands have honed it to perfection.

Fox News repeats slogans across all programming, building a unified narrative that shapes the way millions perceive news events. Apple uses the same vocabulary to describe products through every contact point, from keynotes to packaging to store environments. Geico has maintained its "15 minutes could save you 15% or more" message for over two decades even though it has generated an infinite number of creative alternatives.

Last chapter, we discussed how to write your Core Narrative. This chapter will address the equally critical challenge: how to make that story unavoidable through strategic repetition that burrows your message into the market's awareness.

THE SCIENCE OF MESSAGE PENETRATION

To see why repetition is so effective, we must first witness how information enters awareness in our hyper-mediatic age.

The average consumer today is now faced with between 4,000 and 10,000 brand messages every day. To deal with this flood, our brains use advanced filtering mechanisms that capture the vast majority of the messages before they become consciously aware.

This creates what attention economists refer to as the "Attention Barrier"- a neurological firewall that guards our limited capital of mental energy by screening out most of the input that comes at us.

The marketer's takeaway: **It generally takes 7-27 repetitions of the same message before it breaks through this barrier.**

This is the reason why most marketing attempts fail even with genius creativity. A great message, having been heard, will never be remembered. A dull message, heard twenty times, remembered forever.

However, frequency won't suffice alone. Cognitive psychology research suggests three primary factors on which the effectiveness of repeated messages depends: penetrate or die.

1. Consistency Coefficient

If messages radically differ between exposures, the brain treats each one as new information instead of as reinforcement of previous information. That resets the exposure counter, eliminating cumulative effect.

High consistency coefficient brands maintain message consistency on channels and touchpoints. Language, imagery, tone, and important claims of their brands remain consistent although creative executions may differ.

2. Distinctiveness Ratio

Appears like competition messages, these competition messages neurologically blend with competitor messages to become indistinguishable and produce category noise instead of brand signal. Distinctiveness ratio measures how much does your message clearly move away from the category norm.

Distinctiveness ratio brands possess perceptual territory that's one of a kind distinct from everyone else's and cannot be authoritatively attributed by their competitors and, thus, repeatedly sent-off messages always have a distinctive feel of being entirely theirs alone.

3. Relevance Resonance

Messages aligned with dominant schemas (thought patterns) in the consumer's mind break into awareness in fewer cycles. Relevance resonance captures this awareness of your message alignment with prevailing mental frameworks.

Strongly applicable brands use prevailing belief, values, or knowledge in a way that their messages start to feel familiar even with initial exposures.

Message penetration formula is given as:

MP = R × (C × D)

Where:

- MP is Message Penetration
- R is Repetition Frequency
- C is Consistency Coefficient
- D is Distinctiveness Ratio multiplied by Relevance Resonance

Which is why some campaigns succeed at relatively modest levels of exposure and others tank despite huge investments in the media. Lack of consistency, uniqueness, and salience turns repetition into mere nuisance instead of influence.

THE THREE SYSTEMS OF REPETITION

Repetition does not mean continual repetition of a similar message. Strategic repetition has an effect on three interconnected systems:

1. The Verbal Repetition System

Repetition most clearly includes steady words- the exact language and literal phrases that summarize your Core Narrative.

Political campaigns excel at repetition of language with verbal repetition through message discipline under management:

Building "message calendars" where communications are concentrated on target themes

Producing "talking points" that are distributed to all spokespeople

Preparing representatives to "bridge" any question to central messages

Employing "message reinforcement teams" to enforce discipline through all media

Apple exemplifies mastery of verbal repetition through consistent product phrasing. During the launch of the first iPhone, Steve Jobs called it "revolutionary" and "magical"-

terms repeated by employees, ads, packaging, and sales reps thousands of times over the next few months.

To construct your Verbal Repetition System:

Step 1: Construct your Message Hierarchy

- Primary Message (Central Story in its tightest-knit form)
    - Supporting Messages (3-5 key statements reaffirming the Primary Message)
    - Evidence Points (Individual facts, details or anecdotes which substantiate Supporting Messages)

Step 2: Build your Lexical Framework

- Core Terms (Words that need to be used uniformly)
    - Preferred Terms (Words that can be used when they are available)
    - Avoided Terms (Words that are hurtful to your narrative)

Step 3: Apply Message Control Protocols

- Hierarchical authorization of customer-facing messages
    - Message training of every customer-facing employee
    - Ongoing message audits by every channel

- Message consequence programs

The application of word repetition always has a stifling feel to creative personnel. That tension needs to be resolved by clear instructions on where creativity can be unleashed (implementation) and where consistency is paramount (central messaging).

2. The Visual Repetition System

Whereas verbal repetition operates through language, visual repetition operates through repeated imagery, graphical components, and non-verbal signals.

The most advanced brands have strict visual repetition systems:

- McDonald's golden arches exist with precise color definition worldwide
    - Coca-Cola's dynamic ribbon has precise measurements in every usage
    - Nike's swoosh can be recognized even when taken out of context from other brand components

Political elections illustrate visual repetition through:

- Repeated color schemes used (Republican red, Democrat blue)
    - Same typography on every material

  - Repeated backgrounds and sets throughout events
  - Precise placement of logos

To construct your Visual Repetition System:

Step 1: Build your Visual Hierarchy

- Central Visual Elements (Logo, primary imagery, signature color)
  - Support Visual System (Typography, graphical devices, photograph look)
  - Application Framework (How visual elements change across contexts)

Step 2: Design your Visual Governance Structure

- Master Brand Guidelines (Through regulations for usage of visuals)
- Simplified Use Guides (Easily reachable rules for vendors and partners)
- Templates and Pre-Approved Assets (Facilitators which guarantee compliance)

Step 3: Carry out Visual Compliance Processes

- Brand custodians with power of approval
- Scheduled cycles of visual inspections for every touchpoint
- Systems of templates to apply throughout common usage

- Internal stakeholders and external partners training modules

The optimal visual repetition system achieves a balance between extremely stringent safeguarding of foundational assets and explicit standards for proper development and adjustment throughout environments.

3. The Experiential Repetition System

The most advanced type of repetition transcends what brands say (verbal) and how they appear (visual) to build repeatable experiences with every customer interaction.

Disney is the quintessential experiential repetition with:

- Repetitive cast member terminology ("guests" instead of "customers")
    - Protocolized greeting and service procedures
    - Uniform aesthetic regulation across properties
    - Repeatable emotional trajectories in attractions

Political campaigns build experiential repetition with:

- Protocolized rally formats with repeatable emotional curves
    - Standard volunteer training and talking points

- Standard fundraising and participation experiences

Standard social media interaction patterns

To construct your Experiential Repetition System:

Step 1: Map Customer Experience Touchpoints

- List all points of brand interaction
    - Prioritize these moments by influence and frequency
    - Determine which aspects to standardize vs. adapt

Step 2: Create Experience Standards

- Signature Moments (High-impact interactions that define your brand)
    - Interaction Protocols (Protocols for routine customer interactions
    - Emotional Outcomes (Emotions each interaction should evoke)

Step 3: Build Experience Training and Assets

- Experience playbooks for every department
    - Role-specific training programs
    - Performance measurement linked to experience delivery
    - Recognition programs for outstanding experience providers

When the three systems of repetition all align, your Core Narrative is not only communicated- it's lived out consistently in every brand encounter, creating cumulative impact beyond competitors' reach.

THE STRATEGIC REPETITION FRAMEWORK

Having defined the three repetition systems, now let's discuss the strategic framework for implementing them:

Phase 1: Repetition Audit

Begin by examining your current performance in repetition:

Step 1: Message Consistency Analysis

- Gather all customer-facing materials for the past 90 days
    - Establish the top 5-10 messages being communicated
    - Measure the consistency coefficient (percentage of materials communicating each message)
    - Measure against the consistency pattern of the competition

Step 2: Touchpoint Inventory

- Enumerate all customer touch points (physical, human, digital, advertising)

    - Evaluate consistency of message via these touchpoints
    - Pinpoint high-impact touch points having low message consistency
    - Customer journey map to highlight repetition gaps in repetition

Step 3: Competitive Repetition Audit

- Inspect competitor patterns of message
    - Compute perceptual space they have from repetition
    - Locate competitive repetition weak points
    - Compute your distinctiveness ratio with key competitors

Most organizations will find that their repetition effect is much lower than they estimated. Messages will tend to differ drastically across departments, channels, and time frames, diluting effect and blocking accumulation effect.

Phase 2: Repetition Strategy

Using your findings in your audit, construct your strategic repetition plan:

Step 1: Message Concentration Decision

- Identify lead message for repetition (from your Core Narrative)
    - Establish concentration targets (what

  - percentage of communications to apply this message)
  - Define timeframe for repeated repetition (min. 6-12 months)
  - Define evolution parameters (what is allowed to evolve vs. what stays the same)

Step 2: Channel Prioritization

- Determine high-impact channels for message reenforcement
  - Prioritize repetition resources by channel effectiveness
  - Design channel-specific repetition needs
  - Design cross-channel coordination processes

Step 3: Repetition Calendar Design

- Design message release calendar by channels
  - Identify consistency targets by each time interval
  - Define measurement processes for repetition adherence
  - Define performance measures for message penetration

Most effective repetition methods concentrate resources on a fewer number of messages presented more regularly, rather than attempting to reach all people with all messages.

Phase 3: Repetition System Deployment

Having set your strategy, implement the three repetition systems:

Step 1: Organizational Alignment

- Obtain leadership buy-in to message discipline
    - Build cross-functional repetition governance team
    - Develop consequences for message violation
    - Design incentives for repetition compliance

Step 2: Tool Development

- Build message playbooks in each department
    - Develop templated content expressing core messaging
    - Develop training programs on repetition value
    - Develop approval processes for message consistency

Step 3: Creative Framework

- Develop guidelines for creative expression
    - Establish the non-negotiables of all messages
    - Develop message change rules over time

- Develop processes for creative proposals with message integrity

The tension between message discipline and creative freedom must be balanced through clear guidelines and processes that protect core message integrity but enable new, engaging expressions.

OVERCOMING REPETITION RESISTANCE

Effective repetition's biggest challenge is not outside competition but inside resistance. There are three types of resistance that generally occur:

1. Fatigue

Marketing groups grow tired of messages long before shoppers even become aware of them. This puts pressure on switching directions too quickly, so messages do not get to effective levels of penetration.

Solution: Practice the 10x Rule

If in-house teams are experiencing message fatigue, double the timeline by 10 to estimate when consumers would most likely start to experience fatigue too. Most messages are dropped at the exact time they are just starting to break into consumer awareness.

2. Executive Impatience

Executive impatience reigns when market results don't appear to accrue instantly from repetition efforts, without message influence's cumulative effect being recognized.

Solution: Build Repetition Metrics

Develop mid-term metrics of message penetration beyond sales outcomes, i.e., recall of message, association of brand attribute, and search volume on main phrases. These signal progress prior to financial outcomes being realized.

3. Silos in the Organization

Various departments naturally pay most attention to messages related to their own objectives, resulting in communication fragmentation that prevents any single message from reaching breakthrough.

SOLUTION: ESTABLISH MESSAGE GOVERNANCE

Create a central messaging authority with approval rights department-wide, defined hierarchy of messages, and procedures for maintaining department-specific messaging within the master system.

By confronting these points of resistance beforehand, organizations can uphold the discipline of message that allows for genuine market penetration.

Case Study: GEICO's Mastery of Repetition

GEICO delivers a masterclass in repetition in marketing. It has reused the same overall message of "15 minutes could save you 15% or more on car insurance" in thousands of ads in many different creative campaigns since 1999:

- The GEICO Gecko
    - The Cavemen
    - "Happier Than."
    - "Did You Know."

Whereas the delivery was revolutionary creative, the message remained fundamentally unchanged during more than two decades of duration, driving remarkable message penetration and thus creating GEICO a 2nd largest insurer among the 8th largest initial auto insurers.

Repetition strategy displays some worth-perceiving ideas

- Consistency of the Message and the variety of Execution: Same central message, unlimited creative variety
    - Strategic Message Evolution: Shifting from time savings (15 minutes) to money savings (15%) as the main advantage in reaction to market research
    - Cross-Channel Integration: Message consistency while being respectful of channel-specific demands
    - Long-Term Commitment: Preventing creative team burnout to continue changing direction

The end result is a message so ingrained in consumer awareness that it has achieved the level of cultural speak- the holy grail of strategic repetition.

Conclusion: From Message to Movement

As we reach the end of this chapter, keep in mind that repetition isn't simply a strategic marketing choice- it's the subtle mechanism through which messages become movements.

The most effective brands in the world realize that breakthrough is achieved not by talking about something different, but by talking about something consistent with such consistency that it becomes embedded in the way that people think.

Nike's "Just Do It" wasn't an ad campaign; it was a dedication to message reinforcement that turned a shoe brand into a worldwide phenomenon. Amazon's obsession with customers wasn't a catchphrase; it was an over-and-over-repeated promise reflected through every deed and every message. Trump's "Make America Great Again" wasn't a slogan; it was a focused narrative repeated with such frequency that it struck America's heart.

In the following chapter, we'll explore how to execute your repetition plan more with the Echo Messaging System-intentional execution of your Core Narrative through advertising, content, and social media to generate omnipresent brand presence.

First, consider this: What message are you going to repeat with such relentless consistency that it's not possible for your market to ignore?

6

THE ECHO MESSAGING SYSTEM — EMBEDDING YOUR BRAND EVERYWHERE

Felix Baumgartner climbed into a capsule inside a helium balloon in 2012 and leaped to the edge of space. He wore a pressurized suit when he broke records: he jumped. He plummeted toward the Earth for four minutes and twenty seconds, breaking the sound barrier in his human body, then deployed his parachute and floated gently down into the New Mexico desert.

This was not a NASA mission. It was not a government mission. It was "Red Bull Stratos"- a marketing stunt orchestrated by an energy drink company that had rebranded itself into something far more valuable: the undisputed owner of extreme sports and human performance in the consumer's mind.

The jump was witnessed in person by over 8 million. Coverage on the news channels was watched by some 600 million. The clip-on YouTube has been viewed over 46 million times. All with considerable Red Bull branding in each.

Most strikingly, nobody asked why an energy drink manufacturer was putting a man into the stratosphere. It felt completely natural because Red Bull had invested twenty years of careful seeding its brand into every discussion of extreme sports and human performance boundaries.

This is the power of what I call the Echo Messaging System- the intentional deployment of your Core Narrative across multiple channels, formats, and contexts to create an omnipresent brand presence that makes you the default owner of a specific conversation in the consumer's mind.

In the previous chapters, we explored creating your Core Narrative and making it unignorable through repetition. We now turn our attention to how to leverage this foundation and make it into a full Echo Messaging System that implants your brand in every direction your target looks.

FROM CAMPAIGN THINKING TO CONVERSATION OWNERSHIP

Most brands work on campaigns- defined marketing initiatives with beginning and end dates. Strong brands work on conversations- ongoing dialogue they systematically infiltrate and eventually own.

Red Bull did not develop ad campaigns around action sports. They became action sports. They did not just sponsor events; they created them. They did not just place their logo on content; they built media properties. They did not just partner with athletes; they discovered, developed, and employed them.

The difference matters:

Campaigns speak AT people; Echo Systems speak THROUGH surroundings

Campaigns create short-lived attention; Echo Systems create durable association

Campaigns compete for share of voice; Echo Systems own entire conversations

It is this shift from campaign mindsets to considering ownership of conversation that is the shift to what I would refer to as "Echo Marketing"- the intentional routing of your message through settings which you influence, control, or build.

THE ARCHITECTURE OF AN ECHO MESSAGING SYSTEM

The best Echo Messaging System in the business has four layers that work together:

Layer 1: The Core Narrative Foundation

Centering your Echo Messaging System is your Core Narrative- the fundamental story that informs us about what your brand believes in the market (something we developed in Chapter 4). For Red Bull, the narrative was "giving wings" to human performance, literally and figuratively.

This story must:

- Be simple enough to travel economically through channels
- Be flexible enough to adopt various contexts
- Different enough to create immediate brand recognition
- Consistent enough to have cumulative effect

Your Core Narrative is the gravitational centre around which everything else orbits, delivering consistent brand meaning amid variant expressions and touchpoints.

Layer 2: The Conversation Territory

The second level is the specific conversation your brand will enter systematically and ultimately own. This ground must be:

- Relevant to your product category or value proposition
  - Consistent with your authentic capabilities and values
  - Valuable to your target market
  - Under-served by existing players
  - Long-term development-friendly

Red Bull set "extreme human performance" as their conversation ground- one connected to their product benefits (energy, stimulation, performance) but not as specific as their assigned category (energy drinks).

Declaring your conversation territory requires strategic self-control. It must be narrow enough to own but broad enough to sustain ongoing content and conversations. It's a matter of finding the sweet spot of relevance versus ownership value.

Layer 3: The Channel Ecosystem

The third layer maps out the particular channels, platforms, and environments where your territory dialogue happens. This ecosystem is typically made up of:

Owned Media: Channels that you own outright (sites, social accounts, apps)

Earned Media: Word and coverage that you earn (PR, social share, word of mouth)

Paid Media: Positions that you purchase (advertising, sponsorships, influencer partnerships)

Shared Media: Shared locations (co-created content, forums with community)

Physical Media: Physical spaces (events, shop locations, product experiences)

Red Bull's channel ecosystem is comprised of their owned media realm (Red Bull Media House, Red Bull TV, Red Bull Records), earned media coverage of their events, paid sponsorships, athlete partnerships, and physical events and experiences around the world.

The greatest Echo Systems don't just tap into available channels- they create new ones entirely to amplify their tale in their target area.

Layer 4: The Content Engine

The fourth tier is your process-based approach to creating, curating, and distributing content that reinforces your tale across your territory across your ecosystem. This engine includes:

Content Strategy: The grand plan for what you will create and why

Content Calendar: The planned scheduling of what is on display when

Content Creation Framework: The processes, people, and resources for making it happen

Distribution Protocol: How content moves throughout your universe

Measurement System: How you monitor content performance and storytelling penetration

Red Bull's content engine produces over 5,000 pieces of content annually- from feature films and documentaries to social media shorts, articles, podcasts, and live streams- all capitalizing on their promise of extreme performance.

When these four pillars are aligned, they create a self-perpetuating mechanism that makes your brand ubiquitous in your preferred conversation, positioning you as its natural and rightful owner.

STRATEGIC ECHO MAPPING: FINDING YOUR TERRITORY

The first step to building your Echo Messaging System is finding the right conversation territory to claim. You must take a systematic mapping process:

Step 1: Narrative Expansion

Begin by blowing out your Core Narrative into possible conversation territories:

- What broader human interests connect with our story?
    - What cultural conversations naturally map to our story?
    - What community interests connect with our brand purpose?
    - Which lifestyle elements correspond to our product value?

Brainstorm 10-15 likely areas of conversation that correspond with your Core Narrative. For example, if your narrative is around facilitating creativity (like Adobe), some areas might be digital art, content creation, creative learning, or design thinking.

Step 2: Territory Evaluation

Then, assess each potential territory against five key criteria:

Ownership Potential: How easy is it to become the authoritative voice in this conversation?

High: Little established competition, dispersed current ownership

Medium: Established voices but unknown owner

Low: Land already controlled by established players

Audience Value: How vital is this conversation to your target audience?

High: Fundamental to audience identity and day-to-day concerns

Medium: Relevant but not essential to audience

Low: Marginal to audience identity and issues

Commercial Connection: How strongly does this space connect to your business aspirations?

High: Direct line from conversation to conversion

Medium: Indirect but clear connection to business outcome

Low: Tenuous connection that requires multiple logical leaps

Content Sustainability: Can this space sustain repeated content and activity?

High: Endless topics, shifting developments, high exploration value

High: Important but potentially exhaustible content opportunities

Medium: Limited long-term potential for new, engaging content

Competitive Differentiation: How distinctively can you own this territory compared to competitors?

High: Solely yours by virtue of your brand positioning

Medium: Writable but winnable with continued investment

Low: Shared equally by multiple competitors

Score each potential territory on these five dimensions, and then select the 2-3 highest-scoring possibilities for further analysis.

Step 3: Conversation Analysis

On your highest-scoring areas, conduct a subtle conversation analysis:

- Where exactly is this conversation taking place? (environments, platforms, channels)
    - Who are the today's authority figures? (organisations, brands, people)
    - What kind of content dominates this conversation? (articles, videos, social updates)
    - What are the entry points for new voices to get into the conversation? (up-and-coming platforms, overlooked sub-topics)

- What are the rules for the conversation? (etiquette, credibility signals, language)

This analysis reveals the current state of the conversation and illustrates strategic entry points for penetration and claim.

Step 4: Territory Selection and Definition

Once you've analysed and evaluated, select a primary conversation territory and define it specifically:

Territory Statement: A clear statement of the conversation you will own

Territory Boundaries: The precise areas you will and won't include

Territory Connections: How this conversation connects to your Core Narrative

Territory Indicators: How you'll measure your ownership progress

Red Bull's territory might be: "The conversation around pushing human bodily performance beyond the usual boundaries, centered around action sports, endurance activities, and record-breaking athletic performances, connected to our Core Story of 'giving wings' to the potential of humans."

Having defined your territory, you can begin building the infrastructure for owning it in an intentional manner.

THE ECHO SYSTEM BLUEPRINT: CREATING YOUR INFRASTRUCTURE

Once you've established your conversation territory, you need to create the infrastructure to stake it out. This is a four-step process:

Phase 1: Echo Foundation

Begin by establishing your home base:

Step 1: Build Your Territory Story

Create a rich document that covers:

- Your perspective on the territory conversation
    - Your personal opinion within this conversation
    - The specific sub-topics you will address
    - The value you will add to audience participants

Step 2: Design Your Central Hub

Develop a core destination to serve as your headquarters for conversation:

- A distinct website or content hub
    - A standalone social media presence
    - A video or podcast show
    - A physical location or recurring event

Your hub should be platform-convenient but brand-controlled, where you can create strong ownership signals.

Step 3: Establish Your Content Creation Framework

Develop the building blocks and procedures to support consistent content creation

- Content creation teams (internal, external, or hybrid)
    - Content guidelines (tone, style, formats, quality standards)
    - Production workflows (ideation, creation, approval, distribution)
    - Asset management systems (storage, rights, reusability)

This framework enables you to have consistent territory presence without repeatedly having to reinvent processes for each new piece of content.

Phase 2: Echo Expansion

Next, methodically extend your presence across your chosen ecosystem:

Step 1: Platform Prioritization

Establish and rank channels based on:

Presence of audience (where your target already gathers)

Relevance of conversation (natural fit for your domain)

Potential for ownership (ability to stake claim)

Resource demands (expense, time, skill needed)

Develop a staged strategy to expand across platforms in order of priority, rather than simultaneous conquest.

Step 2: Building Your Network

Discover and engage with top players in your domain conversation:

Subject matter experts and authorities

Creators and influencers of content

Organizers and curators of community

Enthusiasts and end users

Create systematic outreach and partnership programs to involve these players in your Echo System.

Step 3: Developing the Content Ecosystem

Grow your content ecosystem with three types of territory content:

Pillar Content: Big, high-value-production content that creates authority

Documentaries, research reports, annual events, signature series

Example: Red Bull's feature-length documentaries such as "The Art of Flight"

Regular Content: Regular, timetabled content that maintains presence

Podcasts, video series, newsletters, monthly features

Example: Red Bull's athlete profile series and competition coverage

Reactive Content: Responsive, timely content that is demonstrably relevant

News commentary, trend analysis, event coverage, conversations

Example: Red Bull's live sporting event content

This three-layer strategy supports continued presence while permitting planned excellence as well as timely relevance.

Phase 3: Echo Acceleration

Having built your foundation and expansion now under way, push your ownership of territory:

Step 1: Conversation Leadership Initiatives

Move from being a contributor to the conversation to leading it:

- Host industry conferences or events
    - Publish definitive studies or reports
    - Develop awards or recognition schemes
    - Provide education or certification programs

These actions make your brand the natural leader in your domain.

Step 2: Echo Amplification Partnerships

Develop strategic partnerships that extend your reach:

- Media companies for content distribution
    - Technology platforms for reach extension
    - Educational institutions for credibility
    - Partner brands for cross-audience sharing

These partnerships enhance your reach beyond your immediate capabilities.

Step 3: Community Cultivation

Engage your audience as participants:

- Develop contribution mechanisms (user-generated content programs)
    - Develop recognition systems (displayed community member highlights)
    - Establish connection platforms (forums, groups, events)
    - Develop advocacy programs (ambassador initiatives)

As your audience becomes active participants within your Echo System, they amplify your stewardship through their own networks and relationships.

Phase A: Echo Measurement

Throughout all phases, use systematic measurement of your territory ownership:

Step 1: Establish Ownership Metrics

Develop accurate measures of conversation ownership:

- Share of Voice (your portion of total conversation volume)
    - Authority Indicators (citations, references, expert recognition)
    - Search Dominance (ranking for territory-related terms)
    - Audience Association (survey-based measures of brand-territory connection)

Step 2: Construct Measurement Infrastructure

Use systems to track these metrics systematically:

- Social listening tools
- Web analytics configurations
- Search performance tracking
- Ongoing audience research

Step 3: Create Optimization Processes

Create feedback loops to continuously optimize ownership:

- Regular territory analysis reviews
  - Content performance review
  - Channel effectiveness assessment
  - Competitive movement monitoring

This measurement framework enables you to track progress toward territory ownership and adjust strategies as the conversation evolves.

CASE STUDY: RED BULL'S ECHO MASTERY

Red Bull provides the perfect case study on Echo System implementation. Let's see what they do through our lens:

Echo Foundation

Territory Narrative: Red Bull created a distinctive vision for extreme performance centered on edge-cutting innovation, personal courage, and cinematic storytelling.

Central Hub: Red Bull Media House was their content hub, creating over 5,000 items of content per annum and being an actual media company, as opposed to a marketing department.

Content Structure: Red Bull established massive production experience with a combination of in-house teams and specialized partner networks with consistent standards of quality across all output.

Echo Growth

Platform Prioritization: Red Bull systematically expanded from live events through to documentary films, streaming platforms, social media, print magazines, music labels, and mobile apps.

Network Building: They created the Red Bull Athlete Network, contracting over 800 athletes in dozens of sports who participate in content and create their own.

Content Ecosystem: Their three-phase model includes pillar content (feature films like "The Art of Flight"), recurring content (competition series, athlete biographies), and reactive content (live event streaming).

Echo Acceleration

Conversation Leadership: Red Bull created entirely new sports competitions (Red Bull Crashed Ice, Red Bull Air Race) and reinterpreted others (Red Bull Rampage, Red Bull X-Fighters).

Amplification Partnerships: They established distribution partnerships with leading networks, streaming platforms, and media companies to extend their content reach.

Community Cultivation: They cultivated grassroots involvement through Red Bull amateur competitions, training camps, and development programs.

Echo Measurement

Red Bull monitors their ground ownership through blanket measurement of media coverage, social buzz, search leadership, and continuous brand affiliation studies.

The result? When people think about extreme sports and human achievement, they think about Red Bull. Not from advertising in the classical sense, but because Red Bull deliberately embedded itself into every aspect of that conversation with their Echo Messaging System.

BEYOND SCALE: ECHO SYSTEMS FOR ANY BRAND

You might be thinking: "That is great for a brand like Red Bull that has so much resource, but what about the rest of us?"

The principles of Echo Messaging apply to organizations of every size. The answer isn't a lot of resources, but concentration-deciding on a narrow enough conversation space that you can realistically own with resources you have available.

Consider these examples of focused Echo Systems:

Glossier: A beauty firm that built an Echo System about "real beauty for real people" on their Into The Gloss site, user content, and fan-created products.

Barstool Sports: Started as a small publication newsletter before systematically building an Echo System about unfiltered sports talk through podcasts, social media content, and live events.

The Skimm: Began as a small email newsletter before expanding to a full-fledged Echo System for news among millennial women through books, podcasts, and community programs.

Each of them began with limited resources but had recognized a unique conversation they could own, then built the structure methodically to dominate it.

The principles to scale to any size organization:

1. **Narrow Your Territory:** Focus on an extremely narrowly defined subset conversation you can actually own

2. **Start With One Channel:** Learn one platform before scaling

3. **Leverage Community:** Make audience members content creators and brand ambassadors

4. **Partner Strategically:** Utilize partnerships to grow reach without growing resources

5. **Measure Relentlessly:** Direct resources to what demonstrably grows territory ownership

Echo Systems are not about spending more than the competition; they're about outthinking them- finding a conversation space tight enough to own but rich enough to be important.

CONCLUSION: FROM CHANNEL PRESENCE TO CONVERSATION OWNERSHIP

As we conclude this chapter, remember that the greatest brands don't just appear on channels; they own conversations. They don't compete for transient attention; they build enduring connection with particular spaces in the consumer's mind.

Red Bull does not need to convince customers that they make an energy drink; they own the mind space for extreme human performance. When someone thinks of pushing beyond boundaries, Red Bull is the one that comes to mind automatically- not because of advertising but because of systematic Echo Messaging.

Apple does not have to persuade consumers they produce technology; they own design and innovation in the consumer's psyche. When one thinks of stunning, working technology, Apple comes to mind automatically.

Your Echo Messaging System is the doorway between your Core Narrative and market ownership. It makes your message something people naturally think; the ultimate aim of all brand development.

In the next chapter, we'll discover how to expand your Echo System into algorithmic spaces with Algorithm Engineering-teaching search engines and AI platforms to recognize your brand as the default go-to authority in your preferred space.

But first, you need to ask yourself: What conversation can your brand rightfully claim in the minds of your customers? The response to that is where your Echo System begins.

7

ALGORITHM ENGINEERING — TRAINING AI & SEARCH TO FAVOR YOUR BRAND

In 2006, a small software company launched a simple WordPress blog focused on inbound marketing concepts. They published articles about email marketing, lead generation, and content strategy- consistently, methodically, relentlessly.

By 2011, this business had created well over 1,000 blog entries, each carefully optimized around particular keyword phrases. When a person was looking for "inbound marketing," "lead generation," or dozens of surrounding terms, this business ruled the results.

That company was HubSpot. And what they accomplished wasn't just content marketing- it was systematic algorithm engineering. They didn't just create content; they programmed the digital landscape to associate their brand with an entire marketing philosophy.

Today, HubSpot isn't just a software provider- they're the default authority on inbound marketing. When marketers think about the concept, they think about HubSpot automatically. The company engineered this association not just in human minds, but in the algorithms that increasingly shape what humans see, believe, and trust.

We've now entered an era where market perception is mediated through algorithmic systems. Google processes over 8.5 billion searches daily. Meta's algorithms determine what content reaches 3.6 billion users. AI systems like ChatGPT generate responses based on their understanding of authority and relevance. These algorithms aren't neutral observers- they're active participants in market narrative creation.

In previous chapters, we explored building your Core Narrative and implementing your Echo Messaging System. Now we'll examine how to engineer these digital gatekeepers to recognize your brand as the natural authority in your chosen territory, ensuring algorithmic visibility that creates market dominance.

THE ALGORITHM IMPERATIVE: WHY ENGINEERING MATTERS

Before diving into strategy, let's understand why algorithm engineering has become essential to market control:

The Mediated Perception Reality

Today, market perception rarely forms through direct

brand-consumer interaction. Instead, it's mediated through algorithmic systems that determine:

- Which brands appear in search results
- Whose content surfaces in social feeds
- What information AI systems provide when questioned
- Which products receive recommendation priority
- Whose thought leadership gains visibility

When consumers search for solutions, products, or information related to your category, algorithms decide whether your brand appears as the natural authority or remains invisible. In a very real sense, if algorithms don't recognize your authority, you don't have authority in the modern market.

THE FEEDBACK LOOP OF ALGORITHMIC AUTHORITY

Algorithmic visibility creates a powerful feedback loop:

1. Higher search rankings and AI recognition drive more visibility
2. Increased visibility creates more engagement and signals
3. These signals further reinforce algorithmic authority
4. Strengthened authority leads to even greater visibility

This creates a rich-get-richer dynamic where brands that establish early algorithmic advantage compound their dominance over time, making it increasingly difficult for competitors to break through.

THE PERMANENCE ADVANTAGE

Unlike traditional marketing that disappears when campaign funding ends, algorithmic authority creates semi-permanent market position. Once established, it requires significantly less investment to maintain than to build initially, creating a sustainable competitive advantage.

HubSpot's early algorithm engineering continues to pay dividends over a decade later. The authority they established through systematic content creation has become self-reinforcing, requiring competitors to invest disproportionate resources to challenge their position.

This permanence advantage makes algorithm engineering not just a marketing tactic but a fundamental business asset-as valuable to market position as patents or proprietary technology.

THE ALGORITHM ENGINEERING FRAMEWORK

So how do you systematically engineer algorithms to favour your brand? The process follows a four-phase framework:

Phase 1: Authority Mapping

Begin by mapping the specific authority signals that matter in your category:

Step 1: Identify Algorithmic Touchpoints

- Where do customers encounter algorithms in their buying journey?
- Which search terms represent high-value category entry points?
- What questions do they ask AI systems about your category?
- Which social platforms algorithmically surface category content?
- What recommendation systems influence category decisions?

Step 2: Analyse Signal Patterns For each touchpoint, identify the specific signals that algorithms use to determine authority:

Search Engines:

- Content depth and comprehensiveness
- Linking patterns from recognized authorities
- User engagement metrics (click-through, dwell time)
- Branded search volume and associations
- Structured data implementation

Social Algorithms:

- Engagement velocity and sustainability
- Content format and platform alignment
- Community interaction patterns
- Cross-platform signal consistency

- Opinion leader amplification

AI Systems:

- Content volume on definitive sources
- Consistent terminology and framing
- Citation patterns from authoritative sites
- Direct and indirect brand associations
- Expert consensus indicators

Step 3: Competitive Authority Audit

- Who currently holds algorithmic authority in your category?
- What specific signals give them this position?
- Where are the gaps in their authority coverage?
- Which authority dimensions remain unowned?

This mapping process reveals the specific algorithmic landscape you need to engineer to establish market dominance.

Phase 2: Signal Architecture

Next, design the systematic signal patterns you'll create to establish authority:

Step 1: Authority Narrative Development Create a comprehensive document defining:

- The specific expertise territory you'll own
- The key concepts and terms you'll dominate

- The unique perspective that differentiates your authority
- The evidence hierarchy that validates your authority

This narrative becomes the foundation for all content and signal generation.

Step 2: Terminology Engineering Develop the specific language patterns you'll consistently deploy:

- Primary Authority Terms (3-5 phrases you'll completely own)
- Secondary Association Terms (10-15 related concepts you'll link to primary terms)
- Branded Terminology (Proprietary concepts that create unique association)
- Definitional Frameworks (How you'll define and explain category concepts)

These terminology decisions are crucial- they define the specific neural pathways you're creating in both algorithms and human minds.

Step 3: Content Architecture Design the content ecosystem that will generate authority signals:

- Pillar Content (Comprehensive resources that demonstrate complete expertise)
- Supporting Content (Regular publications that reinforce primary authority)
- Engagement Content (Formats optimized for algorithmic distribution)

- Validation Content (Third-party signals that confirm your authority)

This architecture ensures your content doesn't just communicate information but systematically builds algorithmic authority.

Phase 3: Signal Implementation

With your strategy defined, implement the systematic creation of authority signals:

Step 1: Foundation Building Create your authority foundation through:

- Comprehensive pillar content on primary terms
- Structured data implementation
- Technical SEO optimization
- Citation network development
- Branded search volume building

This foundation establishes the basic algorithmic recognition of your expertise.

Step 2: Signal Amplification Expand your authority through systematic amplification:

- Consistent publication cadence
- Strategic linking patterns
- Engagement engineering
- Third-party validation cultivation
- Community signal generation

These amplification activities strengthen the initial authority signals, creating momentum that algorithms recognize and reinforce.

Step 3: Cross-Platform Integration Ensure signal consistency across algorithmic environments:

- Synchronized messaging across platforms
- Cross-platform linking strategies
- Consistent identity signals
- Unified terminology deployment
- Coordinated engagement patterns

This integration multiplies signal impact by creating consistent authority indicators across the digital ecosystem.

Phase 4: Algorithmic Feedback Optimization

Finally, implement systems to continuously optimize your algorithmic position:

Step 1: Signal Monitoring Develop measurement systems to track authority signals:

- Search visibility by term cluster
- Social algorithm distribution patterns
- AI system recognition testing
- Recommendation system inclusion
- Competitive authority shifting

Step 2: Performance Analysis Analyze signal effectiveness through:

- Click pattern analysis
- Engagement quality assessment
- Conversion impact evaluation
- Share of search measurement
- Authority attribution modelling

Step 3: Signal Refinement Continuously refine your authority building based on performance:

- Content optimization for underperforming assets
- Signal gap remediation
- Emerging terminology integration
- Algorithm update adaptation
- Competitive defence mechanisms

This continuous optimization creates a learning system that maintains and extends your algorithmic advantage over time.

REAL-WORLD AUTHORITY ENGINEERING: HUBSPOT'S PLAYBOOK

To see these principles in action, let's analyse how HubSpot engineered algorithmic authority:

Authority Mapping

HubSpot identified that marketers seeking solutions typically began with search, specifically around terms related to lead generation, email marketing, and marketing automation. They noticed these searches often led to disparate, tactical advice rather than cohesive strategy.

Signal Architecture

HubSpot designed a signal architecture around a concept they could own: "inbound marketing." They developed a comprehensive terminology framework including primary terms ("inbound marketing," "lead generation"), secondary associations ("email marketing," "content strategy"), and branded terminology ("attract, convert, close, delight").

Signal Implementation

They implemented this architecture through:

- Creating comprehensive guides on each primary term
- Publishing consistent blog content (3-5 posts weekly for years)
- Developing free tools that generated both value and links
- Building a certification program that created external validators
- Cultivating a partner network that amplified their terminology

Algorithmic Feedback Optimization

HubSpot continuously refined their authority through:

- Regular content audits and updates of existing assets
- Expansion into adjacent terminology territories
- Strategic acquisition of complementary content properties

- Development of topic clusters as search algorithms evolved
- Creation of data-driven content that generated natural backlinks

The result? When you search for "inbound marketing," HubSpot doesn't just appear- they dominate. They own this concept not just in search results but in the broader digital ecosystem. This wasn't accidental- it was engineered through systematic signal creation.

ENGINEERING AI RECOGNITION: BEYOND SEARCH

While search engine engineering has been a focus for years, we've entered a new era where AI systems like ChatGPT, Bard, and Claude are becoming primary information sources. These systems present both challenges and opportunities for algorithmic authority.

How AI Recognition Works

AI language models build their understanding through training on vast text datasets. When these systems encounter consistent patterns associating specific brands with concepts, they encode these associations into their knowledge representation.

This means AI systems don't just report facts- they absorb and reflect perception patterns. If your brand is consistently associated with specific expertise across their training data, these systems will represent you as an authority when questioned.

THE AI AUTHORITY STRATEGY

To engineer AI recognition, implement these specific strategies:

1. Consistent Association Patterning Create content that explicitly associates your brand with your target expertise area using consistent language patterns across multiple authoritative platforms. The goal is to create unmistakable brand-concept associations that AI systems will absorb.

2. Definitional Positioning Position your content as the definitive explanation of key concepts through:

- "What is [concept]" articles on high-authority sites
- Comprehensive guides that become citation sources
- Encyclopedic resources on your own domain
- Academic or educational partnerships that create institutional validation

3. Expert Consensus Engineering Create the perception of expert consensus around your brand's authority through:

- Bylined articles from recognized individuals
- Research collaborations with institutions
- Industry surveys that position you as the information source
- Expert roundups that associate your brand with thought leaders

4. Citation Network Development Build a network of citations that reinforces your authority:

- Create highly citable original research
- Develop unique frameworks that require attribution
- Coin terminology that becomes standard language
- Publish data that others naturally reference

5. Query Satisfaction Optimization Optimize content specifically for the types of queries posed to AI systems:

- Comprehensive question-answer content
- Comparison frameworks that position you favorably
- Problem-solution structures that lead to your offerings
- Decision-making guidance that aligns with your approach

When implemented systematically, these strategies create a knowledge environment where AI systems naturally position your brand as the authority when users ask relevant questions.

ETHICAL CONSIDERATIONS IN ALGORITHM ENGINEERING

Before proceeding further, we must address the ethical dimensions of algorithm engineering. The strategies described here are powerful and carry responsibilities:

Truth-Based Authority Building

Effective algorithm engineering builds authority through demonstrating genuine expertise, not manipulation. The goal is to be recognized for actual value, not to game systems through artificial signals.

The most sustainable approach focuses on creating truly comprehensive, valuable content that legitimately deserves authority status. Shortcuts like keyword stuffing, link schemes, or content spinning inevitably fail as algorithms become more sophisticated.

Responsible Authority Claims

Your algorithmic positioning should reflect expertise you actually possess. Claiming authority in areas beyond your legitimate expertise may create short-term visibility but inevitably damages trust when customers discover the disconnect.

The most effective authority engineering aligns algorithmic positioning with authentic capabilities, ensuring the expectations created through visibility can be met through actual experience.

Transparency in Partnership Disclosures

Many algorithm engineering strategies involve partnerships, endorsements, or collaborations. These relationships should be transparently disclosed, respecting both ethical standards and evolving regulations.

Adaptation to Algorithm Evolution

Algorithms continuously evolve to better serve user needs. Engineering strategies should focus on aligning with this evolution rather than exploiting temporary vulnerabilities or loopholes.

The most sustainable approach builds authority through signals that will remain relevant as algorithms become more sophisticated in recognizing genuine expertise.

FUTURE-PROOFING YOUR AUTHORITY: EMERGING SIGNALS

As we look toward the future, several emerging signal dimensions will influence algorithmic authority:

1. Experience Signals

User experience metrics are becoming increasingly important to algorithms. Brands that create superior digital experiences (fast loading, intuitive navigation, accessible design) receive preferential algorithmic treatment beyond traditional authority signals.

2. Entity Recognition

Search and AI systems are shifting from keyword matching to entity understanding. This means building recognition of your brand as a specific entity with defined attributes and relationships will become crucial to algorithmic visibility.

3. Multimodal Signals

As algorithms evolve to understand images, video, and audio, authority will require consistent signals across all content types. Brands that build authority only through text will find themselves at a disadvantage as these multimodal signals gain importance.

4. Interaction Patterns

How users interact with your content increasingly influences algorithmic understanding. Creating content that generates specific interaction patterns (deep engagement, sharing, saving) will become as important as the content itself.

5. Trust Indicators

As misinformation concerns grow, algorithms are placing greater emphasis on trust signals. Transparent authorship, fact verification, and institutional affiliation will carry increasing algorithmic weight.

By anticipating these emerging signal dimensions, you can build authority that remains resilient through algorithmic evolution.

CONCLUSION: FROM VISIBILITY TO INEVITABILITY

As we conclude this chapter, remember that algorithmic engineering isn't just about visibility- it's about inevitability. The goal isn't simply to appear in search results or AI responses, but to become the inevitable answer when someone seeks information in your category.

When HubSpot engineered algorithms to associate them with inbound marketing, they didn't just gain traffic- they made it nearly impossible to think about the concept without encountering their brand. This created a market position where competitors were forced to either adopt HubSpot's terminology (reinforcing their authority) or use alternative language (limiting their visibility).

In today's algorithm-mediated market, perception isn't just influenced by what customers see, but by the invisible systems that determine what they can see. By systematically engineering these systems to recognize your brand's authority, you create a market position that competitors cannot easily challenge regardless of their marketing budgets.

In the next chapter, we'll explore how to amplify this algorithmic advantage through The Loudest Voice Wins strategy- creating content saturation that drowns out competitive messages and makes your brand the dominant voice in your category.

But first, ask yourself: If algorithms increasingly determine which brands deserve attention, how systematically are you engineering them to recognize yours as the authority?

8

THE LOUDEST VOICE WINS — HOW TO DROWN OUT THE COMPETITION

Three air mattresses on the floor of a San Francisco apartment spawned what would become a $100+ billion company in 2008. By 2022, Airbnb would have booked over 300 million reservations annually, effectively the world's largest hospitality firm without owning a single hotel room.

This was not merely disruptive innovation. It was messaging dominance.

The hotel sector had exponentially greater resources, decades of experience operating, established rewards programs, and enormous advertising budgets. But Airbnb was able to fundamentally shift the way tens of millions of travellers think about where they stay- not by outspending the competition, but by out messaging them.

Where other big hotel brands fought mostly on amenities and reward points, using the standard vocabulary of hospitality, Airbnb relentlessly pounded one message: "Don't stay there. Live there." This message wasn't simply louder than the competition in terms of volume- it was louder in terms of uniqueness, emotional appeal, and platform supremacy.

Airbnb didn't succeed by whispering elsewhere. They succeeded by creating a voice so strong, so unique, and so ubiquitous that the entire discussion of travel lodging started to center around their story instead of the traditional industry's.

In earlier chapters, we discussed creating your Core Narrative, making it impossible to ignore through repetition, planting it everywhere through your Echo Messaging System, and designing algorithms to prefer your brand. Now we'll look at how to build on these components into a Content Saturation Strategy that overwhelms competitive messages and establishes your brand as the loudest voice in your market space.

THE SATURATION IMPERATIVE: WHY THE LOUDEST VOICE WINS

Before diving into strategy, let's understand why content saturation has become essential to market dominance:

The Attention Economics Reality

In today's hyper-fragmented media landscape, attention doesn't divide evenly- it consolidates around dominant voices. This produces a winner-takes-most situation wherein brands that cross the threshold of critical mass of content visibility secure disproportionate mindshare, and brands below the visibility threshold are actually rendered invisible.

A research conducted by the Content Marketing Institute finds that approximately 27% of B2B content receives 90% of attention, while 68% receives virtually zero attention whatsoever. This is not that the invisible content is of low quality- it is just powerless when it comes to saturation.

If your potential customers receive seven messages from your brand to every one from a competitor, you don't have sevenfold influence- you have exponentially. That's because the impact of a message isn't linear to exposure, it follows a power law where key mass generates compounding returns.

Content saturation leads to a psychological effect I term "Perceptual Dominance"- when a brand gains the requisite visibility, consumers perceive it as collectively bigger, more entrenched, and more authoritative than objectively the case.

Airbnb used this effect to great effect. Smaller than the big hotel chains in almost every measurable way (properties, staff, income), their message saturation made it seem like they were the future of travel and that the old hotels were the past.

This change in perception isn't just affecting consumer decision; it's affecting investor sentiment, media narrative, partner choice, and even the approach to regulation. When your voice is leading the narrative, you're not simply altering the way consumers view you- you're altering the way the entire market ecosystem sees your standing.

The Competitive Drowning Mechanism

The strongest feature of content saturation isn't simply that your voice gets heard louder- it's that competing voices become essentially inaudible. It provides a snowballing benefit as competitors struggle more and more to gain message penetration regardless of quality or budget.

Large hotel chains such as Marriott and Hilton were in this predicament because Airbnb flooded the travel discourse. With enormous marketing spend, their message could not break through the Airbnb-dominated discourse. They were not only outspent but also outframed so that their established value propositions came to sound passé irrespective of their inherent value.

THE CONTENT SATURATION FRAMEWORK

So how do you deliberately drown out competing messages? The process takes a four-phase structure:

Phase 1: Conversation Mapping

Start by mapping the particular conversation ecosystems that apply to your market:

Step 1: Identify Conversation Venues

Where do prospects talk about, research, and compare options in your category?

On which platforms do the most influential category conversations take place?

Which sources of information inform decision-making in your market?

Which communities shape perception in your space?

Which media channels are in contact with your consideration target audience?

Step 2: Examine Conversation Patterns

For each location, determine the unique conversation patterns:

Information Channels:

Lead information sources prospects refer to

Opinion-forming authorities trusted

Decision support tools prospects utilize

Evaluation frameworks used on options

Competitive messaging visibility patterns

Community Environments:

Active discussion groups and forums

Opinion-forming community members

Shared questions and concerns

Language patterns and vocabulary

Social proof mechanisms

Media Ecosystems:

Category-influencing publications

Most engaged content formats

Channels of widest reach

Engagement trends across platforms

Points of attention concentration

Step 3: Competitive Voice Audit

Who are the current leaders with the most influential voice in each conversation setting?

What particular messages reign supreme in each setting?

Where are the gaps in the conversations or the underserved topics?

Whose voices are growing or losing influence?

This saturation process uncovers the exact conversational terrain you must fill to achieve voice dominance.

Phase 2: Saturation Strategy

Then, craft your strategic plan for taking over these conversations:

Step 1: Content Dominance Planning

Develop an in-depth saturation strategy outlining:

The exact conversations you'll dominate entirely

The platforms upon which you'll create overwhelming presence

The subjects you'll own conclusively

The content types you'll use at scale

This approach should concentrate resources on owning certain conversational real estate in its entirety instead of having average presence everywhere.

Step 2: Volume Architecture

Build the production framework that will allow content at scale:

Core Content System (How you'll produce foundation pieces)

Expansion Framework (How you'll scale core content across formats)

Distribution Network (How you'll get maximum visibility)

Engagement Mechanisms (How you'll amplify through interaction)

This architecture builds the operational ability to generate content at the volume needed for genuine saturation.

Step 3: Share of Voice Goals

Set voice dominance targets with specificity:

Platform Dominance Metrics (What percentage of relevant content will be yours)

Topic Ownership Goals (Which topics you'll fully dominate)

Conversation Participation Targets (How present you'll be in conversations)

Mindshare Objectives (How you'll quantify perceptual dominance)

These objectives determine what successful saturation means in quantifiable terms, setting clear targets for your execution plan.

Phase 3: Saturation Implementation

Establish your production infrastructure by:

Having your strategy outlined, execute the systematic development of conversational dominance:

Step 1: Content Factory Establishment

Content Creation Teams (Internal, external, or hybrid)

Production Processes (Workflows, approvals, quality control)

Asset Management Systems (Organization, accessibility, reusability)

Scaling Mechanisms (Templates, frameworks, knowledge bases)

This ground builds the capability to create content at saturation levels reliably.

Step 2: Format Diversification

Extend your essential messages into different formats:

- Written Content (Articles, guides, white papers, case studies)

    - Visual Content (Infographics, data visualizations, diagrams)
    - Audio Content (Podcasts, interviews, sonic branding)
    - Video Content (Explainers, tutorials, testimonials, stories)
    - Interactive Content (Tools, calculators, assessments, configurators)

Diversification helps your message penetrate audiences irrespective of content preferences.

Step 3: Distribution Saturation

Put in place thorough visibility on all applicable channels:

- Owned Platform Saturation (Site, email, app, community)
    - Social Platform Domination (Strategic presence on key networks)
    - Third-Party Placement (Guest content, syndication, partnerships)
    - Media Penetration (PR, contributed content, interviews)
    - Community Participation (Forums, groups, comments, discussions)

By this distribution strategy, your message gains omnipresence throughout the entire conversation ecosystem.

Phase 4: Competitive Drowning

Implement specific measures to diminish competitive message visibility:

Step 1: Narrative Preemption

Systematically stake out conversations before others can jump in:

- Develop authoritative pieces on new topics
  - Create terminology that defines the conversation
  - Release master guides that are used as benchmarks
  - Produce proprietary frameworks that influence assessment

This preemption causes competitor messaging to look derivative or incomplete despite their quality.

Step 2: Reframing the Competition

Systematically reframe competitor messaging as out of date or irrelevant:

- Develop comparative content that creates new assessment benchmarks
  - Create "versus" content that dominates the comparison conversation
  - Produce trend content that frames traditional methods as outdated

- Launch studies backing your method over others

This recontextualization alters the ground that conversations are had on by opponents, rendering their messages less compelling even when produced well.

Step 3: Content Surround Strategy

Implement strategies to surround competitor visibility:

- SERP dominance (having multiple results for main terms)
    - Related content suggestions (being seen alongside opponent content)
    - Retargeting campaigns (reaching people after exposure to competitors)
    - Community response presence (being seen in conversations regarding competitors)

This surround strategy guarantees that even when competitors gain visibility, your message is still present in the environment around them.

REAL-WORLD SATURATION SUCCESS: AIRBNB'S PLAYBOOK

To observe these principles in practice, let's examine how Airbnb gained voice dominance over the hotel sector:

Conversation Mapping

Airbnb realized that travel accommodation conversations occurred mainly around:

- Destination search (travel locations, guidebooks, social suggestions)
    - Price search (booking websites, review sites)
    - Experience seeking (social media, travel groups, word-of-mouth)

They saw these discussions often centered on utilitarian factors (location, amenities, price) and not on emotional ones (belonging, authenticity, local experience).

Saturation Strategy

Airbnb built a saturation strategy on reframing lodging as experience:

- Having total control over the "live like a local" discussion
    - Creating pervasive presence on visual channels (Instagram, Pinterest)
    - Holding the domain of real travel experiences
    - Using user-generated content at enormous scale

Saturation Implementation

They executed this strategy by:

- Building the "Airbnb Magazine" as a high-quality content destination
    - Creating "Airbnb Neighborhoods" guides for top destinations
    - Launching the "Experiences" platform with thousands of local experiences
    - Enabling and surfacing host and guest storytelling
    - Creating an enormous library of professional property photos

Competitive Drowning

Airbnb methodically drowned out hotel messaging by:

- Narrative Pre-emption: Defining "authentic travel" before hotels could claim it
    - Competitive Reframing: Positioning hotels as "tourists" vs. Airbnb as "travellers"
    - Content Surround: Creating neighbourhood guides that appeared whenever people researched hotels in popular areas

The outcome? When tourists started making travel plans, Airbnb's "living there" story became the prevailing context in which accommodation choices were measured- rendering conventional hotel messaging about amenities and reward points increasingly irrelevant no matter their real value.

BEYOND VOLUME: STRATEGIC SATURATION PRINCIPLES

Though content quantity is paramount, saturation is really more about applying smart domination within specific conversational space- not mere creation. Such elevated principles define solid saturation vs. mere noise:

1. Message Focus Instead of Dispersion

Effective saturation throws huge amounts of power behind isolated areas of conversational space rather than thin-spraying it all over possible conversation areas.

Airbnb never attempted to compete on business travel or conventions. They focused enormous content efforts on a few conversation spaces (genuine local experiences, one-of-a-kind properties, host connections) until they fully owned these stories.

Implementation Principle: Find the 20% of conversations that drive 80% of decisions in your space and own those totally instead of getting partial presence everywhere.

2. Ecosystem Control Over Content Control

Real saturation doesn't merely regulate what gets spoken, but also the setting where conversations take place.

Airbnb didn't merely produce content for local experiences; they developed the Experiences platform that was the setting where those conversations took place. They didn't merely discuss one-of-a-kind properties; they produced the ultimate presentation that determined the way people discovered and assessed one-of-a-kind places to stay.

Implementation Principle: Whenever feasible, own the sites on which category conversations occur instead of merely engaging in them. Build tools, communities, events, or assets that are the natural habitat of category discussions.

3. Amplification Architecture Over Creation Volume

Innovative saturation builds content for amplification intensity instead of merely generating more pieces.

Airbnb nailed this by developing visual content that was optimized for sharing and amplification. Their home photography wasn't merely informative- it was aspirational, meant to evoke emotional connection and social sharing. Their host narratives weren't merely reviews- they were engaging stories optimized for media attention and social amplification.

Implementation Principle: Craft your essential content with amplification mechanisms built in- features that naturally invite sharing, citation, discussion, and redistribution through both digital and human networks.

4. Perceptual Frameworks Rather Than Factual Claims

The most effective saturation strategies create the mental

frameworks by which all category information is interpreted, as opposed to merely making better claims.

Airbnb not only promised better accommodations, they set the perceptual context that "living like a local" was the superior travel experience. This context then became the metric by which all accommodation choices were measured, instantaneously disadvantaging traditional hotels no matter how good or valuable they were.

Implementation Principle: Use content to set the criteria for category evaluation instead of simply being positioned well within current criteria. Take ownership of how decisions should be made instead of simply why your solution is great.

5. Conversation Sequencing Over Simultaneous Saturation

Strategic saturation acknowledges that market conversations mature through coherent sequences, and dominance involves owning each sequential phase instead of pursuing simultaneous saturation.

Airbnb perfected this ordering by initially dominating the discussion of one-of-a-kind homes and real experiences, then leveraging this ground to shape the next discussion of trust and safety, then both to inform the regulatory debate regarding home sharing.

Implementation Principle: Chart the normal sequence of conversations within your category from awareness to consideration, evaluation, purchase, and advocacy. Create detailed saturation plans for each successive stage, knowing that controlling early conversations gives a head start on later ones.

ETHICAL CONSIDERATIONS IN VOICE DOMINANCE

In finishing up, we need to deal with the ethical aspects of content saturation. The methods outlined above are strong and come with a burden:

Truth-Based Saturation

Effective saturation reinforces real brand truths over falsehoods. Airbnb's supremacy succeeded because their product actually made good on the value proposition of more genuine local experiences- their messaging reinforced a true differentiation, not creating a false one.

Responsible Framing

Although reframing competitor products is tactically advisable, it must be grounded in genuine shifts in point of view and not in deceptive labelling. Airbnb framed hotels as delivering less authentic experiences- a subjective construct many travellers concurred with- as opposed to factually incorrect assertions.

Value-Adding Content

The most sustainable saturation strategies focus on content that delivers real value to audiences, not message repetition. Airbnb's local guides, local experience suggestions, and host stories offered real utility to travellers whether or not they ended up booking on the platform.

CONCLUSION: FROM VOICE TO OWNERSHIP

As we finish this chapter, keep in mind that content saturation is not only about getting heard- it's about becoming the conversation owner. The objective isn't merely to talk more than others, but to so thoroughly own certain conversational real estate that your view becomes the default every thinking through which customers comprehend the whole category.

When Airbnb reached this degree of voice supremacy, they did not simply persuade travelers to use their platform; they revolutionized the way people perceived travel accommodation. The dialogue changed from "which hotel" to "hotel or Airbnb"- and then, for most travelers, to "which Airbnb."

This is the end objective of your Content Saturation Strategy- not only to overpower competitive messages, but to make your brand point of view the go-to conversation starter. When your voice is loud enough, competitors are left reacting to your message instead of creating their own, putting them in a constant defensive posture that renders market leadership virtually impossible to challenge.

In the following chapter, we'll delve into how to take this voice domination to Omnipresence Marketing- making your brand unmissable by making it show up everywhere your people are looking.

But before you do that, ask yourself: If market perception is being more and more influenced by conversational dominance, how methodically are you overwhelming other voices in the conversations that matter most to your business?

9

OMNIPRESENCE MARKETING — MAKING YOUR BRAND IMPOSSIBLE TO IGNORE

In 2011, an annoyed struggling comedian and marketing strategist Michael Dubin was annoyed at the prohibitive cost and unnecessary convolutions of buying razors. Rather than simply grumble about it, he used $35,000 of his own capital and co-founded Dollar Shave Club with friend Mark Levine. What happened next would shake up a hundred-year-old industry controlled by the behemoths in a basic manner.

With almost no advertising budget to Gillette's $800 million-a-year marketing machine, Dollar Shave Club cornered 15% of the market in five years. In 2016, Unilever acquired the company for a staggering $1 billion- all without Dollar Shave Club ever turning a profit.

This wasn't merely clever marketing. It was omnipresence marketing.

Last chapter, we discussed how content saturation makes your brand the noisiest in the room. This chapter takes this a level further: making your brand appear everywhere at all times- an inescapable presence that fundamentally changes consumer thinking and behaviour.

BEYOND VISIBILITY: THE OMNIPRESENCE IMPERATIVE

Classic marketing minds have long centered on reach and frequency. Yet in the current hyper-fragmented attention economy, even great reach across channels can make your brand feel sporadic and unremarkable. Omnipresence marketing is based on an entirely different principle: the illusion of complete market saturation.

The Omnipresence Effect

Studies by the Ehrenberg-Bass Institute show that brands showing up in several contexts at once produce an amplified sense of their market presence. When consumers see a brand across different touchpoints within a condensed time frame, they view that brand as much larger and more powerful than its real market position would indicate.

This mental fallacy, which I term the "Omnipresence Effect," produces a strong market distortion. A company with 10% market share but 90% omnipresence is usually treated by consumers, the media, and even competitors as the category leader.

Dollar Shave Club effectively leveraged this phenomenon. Though it was a mere fraction of Gillette's size, its deliberate omnipresence created the perception of being an industry giant overnight. Its burst viral video (27 million views on a

$4,500 budget), in combination with monthly physical product shipments from their subscription model, helped create a perceived market dominance many times larger than its real territory.

The Cognitive Foundations of Omnipresence

In order to realize why omnipresence marketing is so powerful, we must consider three mental mechanisms:

1. Availability Bias

People vastly overestimate how common what they can readily remember is. When your brand shows up in multiple contexts over a condensed period, customers automatically overestimate your presence in the market.

2. Familiarity Principle

The more frequently people encounter something, the more they tend to prefer it. Omnipresence creates automatic preference through sheer repetition across contexts.

3. Social Proof Compression

When consumers see your brand in multiple venues simultaneously, they unconsciously assume many others must be engaging with it as well, triggering bandwagon effects.

Dollar Shave Club triggered all three mechanisms. Their viral video caused huge availability. Their subscription model provided sustained physical presence. Their social media saturation used user reviews to build dense social proof. The outcome seemed like an overnight shave revolution, even though it was a small company by old-fashioned measures.

The Omnipresence Framework: From Voice to Ubiquity

Based on our Content Saturation Strategy in Chapter 8, let's explore how to build omnipresence systematically throughout your market:

Phase 1: Experience Mapping

Start with mapping all potential experiences where prospects may run into your category:

Step 1: Journey Mapping

What are the total journeys customers follow when considering your category?

What questions do they ask along the way?

Where do they look for those answers?

What influencers influence their thinking?

What is their emotional condition?

Step 2: Context Identification

For each journey point, list all conceivable contexts:

Physical settings applicable to your segment

Online settings where consideration occurs

Social settings where recommendation takes place

Media settings where focus resides

Buy settings where purchase decisions occur

Step 3: Touchpoint Inventory

Develop an exhaustive inventory of every conceivable touchpoint:

Sources of information (sites, reviews, media)

Social touchpoints (sites, groups, influencers)

Physical Touchpoints (retail, events, packaging)

Service Touchpoints (support, usage, renewal)

Relationship Touchpoints (follow-up, community, advocacy)

Dollar Shave Club's mapping showed that while the established razor brands were dominating retail shelf space and sponsoring sports events, they were neglecting key digital touchpoints, subscription experiences, and real male grooming conversations.

Phase 2: Omnipresence Strategy

Second, develop your strategic plan for establishing total category presence:

Step 1: Presence Prioritization

Determine the most impactful presence opportunities:

High-visibility touch points with low competitive presence

Emotionally relevant moments in the customer journey

Decision-critical contexts underserved today

Platform opportunities with natural amplification mechanisms

Physical-digital bridge points with reinforcing effects

Step 2: Synchronization Planning

Create a synchronized omnipresence calendar:

Coordinated sequences of launch across platforms

Reinforcement scheduling between touch points

Compressed-timeframe saturation events

Sustained maintenance planning for presence

Recovery plans for gaps in presence

Step 3: Amplification Architecture

Architecture your presence to amplify itself through:

Viral-optimized content engineering

Incentive structures for social sharing

Cross-platform reinforcement mechanisms

Collaborative amplification partnerships

Community-driven distribution systems

Dollar Shave Club focused on YouTube (underutilized by its competitors), direct-to-consumer subscription (removing retail intermediaries), and genuine male discussions (opposed to Gillette's aspirational communications). They aligned their viral video with subscription launches and reinforced through smart referral programs.

Phase 3: Omnipresence Development

Having your strategy outlined, create the assets and infrastructure necessary for omnipresence

Step 1: Content Ecosystem Development

Develop interlinked content systems for omnipresence:

- Core Brand Assets (video, visuals, messaging, sounds)
    - Platform-Optimized Variants (formatted for every environment)
    - Journey-Stage Content (specific customer phase addressed)
    - Contextual Adaptations (specific environments addressed)
    - Interconnected Asset Networks (establishing mutual reinforcement)

Step 2: Presence Infrastructure

Construct the working backbone for upholding omnipresence:

- Content Distribution Systems (scheduling, publishing, monitoring)
- Presence Management Protocols (frequency, timing, rotation)
- Cross-Platform Coordination Mechanisms (synchronized appearances)
- Presence Measurement Frameworks (visibility, perception, impact)

- Rapid Response Capabilities (opportunity exploitation, gap filling)

Step 3: Physical-Digital Integration

Build smooth bridges between physical and digital presence:

- Physical Products as Media Channels (packaging as content)
- Digital Extensions of Physical Experiences (QR, AR, apps)
- Online-to-Offline Continuity Elements (consistent motifs)
- Experience Synchronization Components (timed revelations)
- Omnipresence Reminder Mechanisms (persistent brand signals)

Dollar Shave Club brilliantly developed their ecosystem of irreverent video content, repurposed it on every platform, and leveraged their physical product (with strategically branded packaging) as a monthly nudge reminding their presence.

Now execute your omnipresence strategy for maximum effect:

Step 1: Synchronized Launch

Launch synchronized presence on all platforms:

Phase 4: Omnipresence Activation

- Concurrent Multi-Platform Deployment (launching everywhere all at once)
- Staged Revelation Sequencing (building up anticipation across touchpoints)
- Cross-Referencing Mechanisms (each presence point pointing back to others)
- Attention Compression Strategies (condensing visibility within narrow time spans)
- Opening Saturation Strength (maximum visibility at opening)

Step 2: Sustained Omnipresence

Sustaining regular presence throughout the ecosystem:

- Presence Rotation Systems (rotating content to keep fresh while sustaining frequency)
    - Gap Analysis Procedures (finding and filling presence gaps)
    - Competitive Displacement Strategies (claiming spaces competitors try to enter)
    - Omnipresence Maintenance Funds (allocated for regular visibility)
    - Presence Refresh Mechanisms (refreshing without breaking continuity)

Step 3: Expansion and Evolution

Expand your omnipresence footprint continually:

- Category Adjacent Expansion (adapting to adjacent conversations)
    - New Platform Colonization (moving into new channels)
    - Experience Extension (providing additional touchpoints to the experience)
    - Presence Depth Enhancement (enhancing depth of existing touchpoints)
    - Omnipresence Innovation (inventing new presence mechanisms)

Dollar Shave Club began with their signature video but soon grew to include podcasts, social media, and groundbreaking packaging. They sustained omnipresence by having a constant presence every month and moved into nearby men's grooming products, which solidified their ubiquity.

REAL-WORLD OMNIPRESENCE: DOLLAR SHAVE CLUB'S PLAYBOOK

To observe these principles in the wild, let's take a look at how Dollar Shave Club built market-distorting omnipresence:

Experience Mapping

Men's shaving experiences were the focal point around which Dollar Shave Club focused,

- Anger at high prices and retail buying

- Discontent with overengineered features
- Neglected replacement cycles causing stale razors
- Disconnection with perfectionist sports messaging

They found touchpoints that established brands were forsaking:

- Genuine male humour as opposed to idealized masculinity
    - Subscription convenience as opposed to retail buying
    - Straightforward value as opposed to feature-laden products
    - Real conversation as opposed to aspirational imagery

Omnipresence Strategy

Dollar Shave Club developed an omnipresence strategy on authenticity and simplicity:

- Prioritizing online video where Gillette was underrepresented
    - Developing a genuine voice lacking in the category
    - Creating a physical product that came monthly as a reminder of the brand
    - Developing a member community as opposed to transactional buying

Omnipresence Development

They implemented this strategy by:

- Their iconic viral video that established the brand voice
    - Packaging that continued the dialogue monthly
    - Email marketing that kept people engaged between shipments
    - Social content that made the brand front-of-mind every day
    - Referral programs for members that amplified presence organically

Omnipresence Activation

Dollar Shave Club activated omnipresence by:

- The explosive release of their viral video
    - Instant sign-up opportunities to subscribe
    - Regular monthly physical product delivery
    - Expansion into neighbouring men's grooming products
    - Corporate messaging that continued to use their irreverent tone

The payoff? In five years, Dollar Shave Club had gained 15% of the U.S. razor market share. Their brand name felt absolutely inescapable without spending a fraction of what Gillette spent on mainstream advertising. When customers thought of razors, Dollar Shave Club had made itself an instant inclusion in the consideration set- not because they spent more than Gillette, but because they achieved omnipresence.

BEYOND FLOODING: STRATEGIC OMNIPRESENCE PRINCIPLES

While omnipresence needs high presence, it's not just about showing up everywhere. These sophisticated principles set strategic omnipresence apart from marketing deluge:

1. Contextual Relevance Rather Than Raw Frequency

Real omnipresence is not about showing up with the same message everywhere. It's about showing up with the appropriate message in every given context.

Dollar Shave Club didn't just bomb their viral ad on every possible channel. They honed their irreverent tone for each one: packaging inserts carried on the conversation in a different way than email or social media posts, but all distinctly felt like Dollar Shave Club.

Implementation Principle: Identify the unique user mindset within each context and tailor your essential message accordingly, while ensuring unambiguous brand consistency through voice, visuals, or conceptual threads.

2. Experience Spans Overloaded Appearances

Strategic omnipresence makes overt links between otherwise disparate touchpoints, creating a unified experience instead of discrete encounters.

Dollar Shave Club effectively bridged the physical-digital gap. Their digital content directly alluded to what members would encounter in their monthly package. Their packaging continued the conversations initiated in emails. Their member feedback influenced future products, creating a cyclical process of engagement.

Implementation Principle: Create intentional paths and cross-references among touchpoints so that every experience refers to and builds upon others instead of standing alone.

3. Asynchronous Coordination Over Simultaneous Bombardment

Advanced omnipresence synchronizes touchpoints over time to make the greatest impact, instead of just showing up everywhere at once.

Dollar Shave Club timed their messages perfectly. Pre-shipment emails-built anticipation. Physical products contained surprises. Post-delivery emails offered tips for use. Social content responded to ongoing member dialogue. Each touchpoint added to the last without repeating it.

Implementation Principle: Create a temporal plan that aligns touchpoints through time, building resonance and momentum instead of wearing out attention all at once.

4. Ecosystem Presence Over Platform Accumulation

The most successful strategies of omnipresence are centered around owning entire ecosystems instead of accumulating presence on disconnected platforms.

Dollar Shave Club didn't just add channels- they developed an entire ecosystem around men's grooming. Their subscription model, content, community, and product line functioned as a coherent system where every component supported each other, not as individual marketing channels.

Implementation Principle: Target omnipresence efforts toward building integrated ecosystems in which your brand becomes a connective tissue, not merely adding more isolated presence points.

5. Memory-Optimized Presence Over Exposure Volume

Strategic omnipresence architecting each touchpoint to optimize memorable impact instead of just optimizing exposure.

Dollar Shave Club made sure each touchpoint had a memorable aspect- from the unexpected humor in their commercials to the witty copy on their packaging to the surprise inserts in monthly shipments. Each left disproportionate memory impressions relative to their competitors' more costly but forgettable communications.

Implementation Principle: Engineer individual memory hooks into every presence point, optimized for recall influence over and above mere exposure, and have those memory elements link to your primary brand story.

ETHICAL CONSIDERATIONS IN OMNIPRESENCE

Just as with any effective strategy, omnipresence marketing involves ethical considerations:

Value-Driven Presence

Ethical omnipresence offers real value at every touchpoint instead of simply interrupting. Dollar Shave Club's omnipresence worked because every touchpoint offered something of value- humour, convenience, savings, or useful grooming tips.

Honesty in Perception

Whereas omnipresence by nature generates a heightened sense of your position in the market, good practice shies away from making false claims of your size or scope. Dollar Shave Club never said they were larger than they were- they just created a presence that made them perceive themselves as being larger.

Respect for Attention

Relevant omnipresence honours user notice instead of flagrantly exploiting it. Dollar Shave Club prudently tuned their communication intensity, making sure they were a welcome presence in their customers' lives and not an intrusive or irritating one.

CONCLUSION: FROM EVERYWHERE TO ESSENTIAL

As we finish up this chapter, keep in mind that the ultimate aim of omnipresence marketing is not to be everywhere- it's to become part of the fabric of how consumers experience and think about your category.

When Dollar Shave Club did reach true omnipresence, they didn't simply take market share; they fundamentally changed the way men considered shaving. The dialogue moved from technology and features to simplicity and value. The buying habit moved from retail to subscription. The connection moved from transactional to membership.

This is the ultimate expression of omnipresence achievement- when your brand not only shows up everywhere but actually redefines the way the whole category is perceived and talked about. When your presence becomes so total that customers are unable to conceive of the category without you, no matter what your actual market size or history.

In the next chapter, we'll consider how to make this omnipresence permanent domination through ecosystem design- creating cross-linked product, service, and experience networks that cement your place in the market.

Before you proceed, try this: If perception increasingly defines market reality, how thoroughly have you designed your brand to not only be visible, but seemingly unavoidable to those customers you desire to serve?

10

PERCEPTION HACKING — CONTROLLING WHAT PEOPLE SAY ABOUT YOUR BRAND

In 1995, when Jeff Bezos launched Amazon as an online bookstore, incumbent players like Barnes & Noble barely even noticed. By 2022, Amazon was a $1.5 trillion behemoth, and Barnes & Noble had dwindled to a shadow of its former self. While all credit Amazon's success to technology innovation and ruthless execution, something more subtle was at work: a brilliant management of brand perception.

Bezos understood something simple that too many business leaders end up forgetting somebody else publicly commenting on your business is infinitely more valuable than you commenting about it. Since the beginning of Amazon, Bezos has been laser-like in his intent to craft the story that would radiate organically from the customer experience, famously stating, "If you make customers unhappy in the physical world, they might each tell six friends. If you make customers unhappy on the Internet, they can each tell 6,000 friends."

But Bezos wasn't just shying away from bad word-of-mouth. He was deliberately designing good stories. Each move- from the 1-Click ordering patent to the development of Amazon Prime to the constant emphasis on customer reviews- was calculated not only to make the business better but to dictate what stories customers would naturally share about Amazon.

This wasn't just excellent customer service. It was perception hacking.

Early in the history of e-commerce, most online stores were preoccupied with transaction efficiency- getting the buying process as slick as possible. But Bezos knew that perceptions of customers would ultimately decide market champions. Competitors were optimizing for conversion rates and basket sizes, but Amazon was optimizing for perception formation- crafting every touchpoint not only for its direct business effect but for its role in the stories customers would tell.

In earlier chapters, we discussed making your brand the loudest voice in your marketplace and building omnipresence to have your brand be omnipresent. Here, we will look at how to leverage the strongest voice of all: that customers have about your business. We will discuss the science and strategy behind perception hacking- the intentional designing of the story's customers tell one another about your business.

Word-of-mouth has always been a powerful force in traditional marketing. But perception hacking works at a more fundamental level: it's about methodically designing the narratives that organically arise out of your brand experience.

THE PERCEPTION ECONOMY

Studies by the Keller Fay Group indicate that the average consumer talks about particular brands in conversation 90 times per week. When each of these conversations drives purchasing decisions by 200-2000% more than paid media, we've entered what I refer to as the "Perception Economy"- where brand perception shared through organic conversation is the most valuable currency.

This change has been hastened by online platforms. What was once fleeting talk is now forever recorded, searchable, and amplifiable. One customer's opinion can reach millions, lingering forever in the digital record.

The consequences are deep. In earlier economic periods, market standing was largely established by distribution dominance, price benefit, or feature excellence. In the Perception Economy, these familiar strengths can be made nearly inconsequential by perception dominance. Businesses with better products but poorer perception engineering frequently struggle against rivals who excel at narrative development.

Think about how many times you've heard someone excuse an Amazon purchase even though they know they could get the same thing elsewhere: "I just trust Amazon more." This feeling of trust- carefully cultivated through thousands of small experience choices- tends to overcome price benefits from competitors.

Amazon saw this change coming early. Instead of attempting to drive the conversation with conventional brand messaging, Bezos set out to design the product experience to create certain, strategic stories. When customers got packages sooner than they expected, were surprised by friendly customer service, or found unexpectedly low prices, they didn't merely feel satisfied- they told stories that supported precisely the brand impressions Amazon wanted to spread.

THE NARRATIVE TRANSFER MECHANISM

To see how perception hacking works so effectively, we must explore three primary mechanisms:

1. Experience-to-Narrative Conversion

Humans are born to be storytellers and naturally transform experiences into narratives to share with others. Any customer interaction with your brand becomes a potential narrative, with some elements being highlighted and others lost depending on emotional resonance and expectation violation.

2. Social Currency Exchange

Individuals tell brand stories not so much to benefit the brand, but for self-social enhancement. Those stories which offer social currency- presenting the teller as being informed, useful, or perceptive- pass on much more quickly and far more extensively than do non-social currency stories.

3. Narrative Persistence

Once a brand story gains traction in the marketplace, it has remarkable staying power, continuing to be shared even long after the originating experience has evolved. This offers opportunity (good stories persist) and danger (bad stories persist as well).

Amazon expertly leveraged all three mechanisms. They designed customer experiences precisely to create stories worth telling (quick shipping, unexpected customer service, huge selection). They made sure these stories had social currency (customers feeling smart for finding great deals or convenient solutions). And they reinforced their core stories through every touchpoint to create amazing persistence.

THE PERCEPTION HACKING FRAMEWORK: FROM EXPERIENCE TO NARRATIVE

Building on the foundation laid in previous chapters, let's examine how to systematically engineer the stories customers tell about your brand:

Phase 1: Narrative Mapping

Begin by mapping the current and potential narratives surrounding your brand:

Step 1: Current Narrative Capture

- What stories do customers currently tell about your brand?
- Which narratives appear most frequently in reviews and social media?
- What emotional themes dominate these stories?
- What particular experiences are most shared by narratives?
- How are stories different among customer segments?

Step 2: Competitive Narrative Analysis

- What are the stories that your competitors hear?
- Whose competitor stories share the highest velocity?
- What narrative holes exist in your space?
- What competitor stories indicate vulnerabilities?
- What narrative real estate is up for grabs?

Step 3: Strategic Narrative Identification

- What stories would best move your business forward?
- Which stories support your strategic positioning?
- Which stories will deliver the highest level of competitive differentiation?
- Which stories would evoke the most valuable customer behaviour?
- What stories hold the highest sharing potential power?

When Amazon did this mapping in its infancy, they found that physical bookstores created stories about discovery browsing and staff picks. Online rivals elicited stories about saving money but were plagued by stories about impersonal service and late shipping. Bezos saw the narrative gap: no store had stories about maniacal customer obsession, huge selection, and unexpected convenience.

Phase 2: Experience Engineering

Then, intentionally craft experiences that will create your target stories:

Step 1: Narrative-to-Experience Conversion

- What particular experiences would naturally create your target stories?
- Which touchpoints hold the most narrative-generating potential?
- What expectation violations would create the most compelling stories?
- Which emotional highs would be most memorable and shareable?
- What signature moments could become definitional to your brand?

Step 2: Narrative Acceleration Elements

Embed specific elements that drive narrative sharing:

- Surprise (strategic surprise moments)
- Noteworthiness (aspects deserving note)
- Social Value (status-granting findings)

- Cues (environmental prompts that trigger retelling)
- Emotional Highs (peak feeling moments)
- Usefulness (useful information worth sharing)

Step 3: Experience Orchestration

Craft the full experience journey to deliver greatest narrative impact:

- Narrative Sequence Planning (sequencing experiences for greatest impact)
- Contrast Engineering (instituting intentional contrasts that increase perception)
- Peak-End Optimization (optimizing intensity of emotional peaks and endings)
- Memory Marker Formation (creating strong memory markers)
- Story Retelling Ease (making narratives simple to retell and share)

Amazon systematically designed its customer experience around narrative creation. They created surprise through "anticipatory shipping" (shipping products prior to customers ordering them). They constructed remarkability through their "everything store" assortment. They created social currency through reviews from customers. They crafted triggers through unique packaging. They amplified emotions through exceed-expectations delivery timing. And they delivered practical value through extensive product information and useful recommendations.

Phase 3: Narrative Infrastructure

Having developed narrative-generating experiences, develop the infrastructure to record and amplify these stories:

Step 1: Narrative Capture Systems

Construct systems to gather and organize customer stories:

- Review Ecosystems (systematic narrative collection)
- Testimonial Generation Processes (eliciting stories at moments of peak emotion)
- Social Listening Infrastructures (listening for stories across platforms)
- Customer Narrative Research (asking probing questions for rich stories)
- Frontline Narrative Collection (empowering employees to recognize compelling stories)

Step 2: Narrative Amplification Networks

Develop infrastructure to strategically scale individual narratives:

- Owned-Channel Highlighting (highlighting customer stories at your properties)
- Influence Network Cultivation (partnering with narrative amplifiers)
- Community Story Exchange (making it easy for customers to share with each other)
- Social Proof Concentration (gathering narratives for maximum visibility)

- Narrative Syndication Programs (spreading stories across channels)

Step 3: Ongoing Narrative Optimization

Create processes for continuous narrative tuning:

- Narrative Effectiveness Measurement (measuring sharing and effectiveness)
- Story Evolution Management (revitalizing and updating master narratives)
- Counter-Narrative Neutralization (managing negative storytelling)
- Narrative Consistency Enforcement (aligning all touchpoints with core stories)
- Narrative Innovation Processes (creating new potential story directions)

Amazon constructed arguably the most advanced narrative infrastructure in the history of business. Their review system trapped more than a billion customer stories. Their "was this review helpful?" functionality brought forward the most engaging stories. Their recommendation engine built tailored stories. Their customer service force was enabled to create "above and beyond" stories. And their ongoing measurement enabled ongoing narrative optimization.

Phase 4: Narrative Propagation

Finally, strategically seed your engineered stories across the marketplace:

Step 1: Narrative Seeding

Place initial iterations of your target narratives in strategic locations:

- First Impression Engineering (managing narrative-defining first experiences)
- Influence Priority Access (providing narrative amplifiers with early experience)
- Strategic Narrative Placement (placing stories in high-visibility situations)
- Demonstration Case Development (developing exemplary narrative examples)
- Narrative Pattern Establishment (establishing recognizable story templates)

Step 2: Story Velocity Acceleration

Operate strategies to accelerate narrative sharing:

- Sharing Incentive Systems (rewarding narrative distribution)
- Story Simplification Processes (simplifying stories to make them easier to repeat)
- Narrative Visualization Creation (making stories real and tangible)
- Retelling Opportunity Engineering (engineering contexts to share stories)
- Narrative Evolution Tracking (tracking how stories evolve as they travel

Step 3: Narrative Reinforcement

Reinforce your target stories repeatedly over time:

- Experience Consistency Management (ensuring stories remain true)
- Ongoing Narrative Validation (fresh evidence for known stories)
- Counter-Narrative Management (managing rival stories)
- Narrative Refreshment Cycles (making established narratives seem new)
- Deep Narrative Integration (seeding stories in company operations and culture)

Step 4: Institutional Narrative Adoption

Take your narrative out to industry infrastructure:

- Media Relationship Development (building relationships with journalists who use your framing)
- Analyst Education Programs (educating industry analysts to perceive through your eyes)
- Academic Partnership Creation (supporting research that supports your narrative)
- Industry Standard Influence (influencing how your category is officially tracked)
- Regulation Framework Engagement (shaping the way your industry is regulated)

Amazon excelled at institutional narrative adoption by having industry analysts start tracking e-commerce success with Amazon's preferred measurement (customer happiness over short-term profitability), academia researched the "Amazon effect" in business courses, and the media repeatedly portrayed retail innovation in terms of Amazon's customer-centric approach.

Amazon's story seeding excellence is seen in the way they planted customer obsession stories through Jeff Bezos's own messages, speeded up velocity by showcasing remarkable customer service anecdotes, and solidified stories through decades of consistent experience delivery. When Bezos took an empty chair to meetings to symbolize "the customer," he wasn't merely building internal culture- he was designing a story that would spread throughout the marketplace.

REAL-WORLD PERCEPTION HACKING: AMAZON'S PLAYBOOK

To observe these principles in practice, let's explore how Amazon perception-hacked its way to being inseparable from customer obsession:

Narrative Mapping

Amazon recognized the retail industry was creating mostly negative stories:

- Frustration due to limited choice and out-of-stocks
- Disappointment in shipping delays and unreliable timing
- Irritation with inconvenient return processes and poor service
- Confusion whether prices were fair or competitive

They discovered narrative territory no competitor owned:

- The feeling of unlimited possibility from endless selection
- The surprise of receiving items faster than expected
- The relief of hassle-free, no-questions-asked returns
- The satisfaction of transparent and consistently low prices

Experience Engineering

Amazon deliberately engineered experiences to generate these narratives:

- "Earth's biggest selection" positioning created remarkability
- Two-day Prime shipping violated expectations (now accelerated to same-day)
- "One-click" ordering removed friction in ways worth mentioning
- Clear customer reviews created unforeseen trust
- Easy returns generated contrast to normal retailing experiences

Narrative Infrastructure

They developed complex infrastructure to gather and amplify these stories:

- Customer review infrastructure that expanded to more than a billion reviews

- "Was this review helpful?" functionality to bring forth the most effective stories
- Recommendation engine that built personalized "discovered for you" stories
- Customer service team authorized to create "above and beyond" stories
- Shareholder letters each year that reaffirmed customer obsession stories

Narrative Spread

Amazon deliberately spread these stories through:

- Bezos's consistent communication of customer obsession
- The vacant chair at meetings for "the customer"
- Press coverage of unusual customer service instances
- Repeated experience delivery solidifying stories across decades
- Scaling customer-centric policies into every new business category

The outcome? When people consider Amazon, the prevailing stories aren't of its technological advanced nature or its enormous size- they are stories of customer fanaticism, ease, and trust. Even when criticized on other dimensions, these underlying stories hold so firmly true that they define the brand in people's minds.

BEYOND MANAGEMENT: STRATEGIC PERCEPTION PRINCIPLES

While perception hacking involves methodically designing experiences, it's more than just managing reputation. Such cutting-edge principles set actual perception hacking apart from traditional strategies:

1. Narrative Generation Rather Than Narrative Control

Real perception hacking doesn't aim at controlling what others say but generating experiences so strong that people organically share your desired stories.

Amazon never asked customers to describe how customer-focused they were. Instead, they designed experiences so unexpectedly customer-focused that these stories developed naturally. When a customer service representative spent hours assisting someone in finding a product Amazon did not even carry, the resultant story traveled much further than any corporate communication ever could.

Implementation Principle: Design signature experiences that are so remarkable they automatically generate stories aligned with your strategic narrative, without needing to explicitly tell customers what to say.

2. Expectation Violation Over Expectation Meeting

The most powerful narratives emerge not from meeting expectations but from strategically violating them in meaningful ways.

Amazon knew this well. When they introduced Prime, two-day shipping broke customer expectations in a big way. When competitors later matched up, Amazon broke expectations once again with same-day and two-hour shipping. Each break created new waves of story-telling that mere expectation-fulfillment could never create.

Implementation Principle: Find specific customer expectations you can break in big ways in a positive manner, keeping in mind that stories are created most strongly out of the space between expectation and experience.

3. Narrative Infrastructure Over Narrative Campaigns

Successful perception hacking creates permanent narrative generation systems instead of short-term campaigns for message delivery.

Amazon's review system is the ultimate expression of this concept. Instead of launching campaigns on trustworthiness, they created an infrastructure that generated trustworthiness stories continuously through real customer voices, providing a permanent flow of new, credible stories.

Implementation Principle: Invest in long-lasting systems that continually create and amplify customer stories instead of campaigns that briefly increase message visibility.

4. Memory Engineering Over Message Engineering

The most advanced perception hacking is concerned with engineering what customers will remember and share, not what they will hear for a brief moment.

Amazon excelled at memory engineering with their unique packaging, surprise delivery timing, and hassle-free returns. Each of these features was crafted not only for the sake of operational effectiveness but also for optimal memorability and sharability, such that what people remembered and passed on exactly corresponded to Amazon's strategic narratives.

Implementation Principle: Create experiences with careful forethought as to what will be most memorable and shareable, understanding that memory distortion patterns are avoidable and can be intentionally exploited.

5. Coherence Management Over Consistency Management

Strategic perception hacking guarantees experiences have a coherent narrative across touchpoints instead of just sustaining consistency of messages.

Amazon did not just maintain consistent messaging- they created a coherent story that played out along the entire customer experience. From the huge selection while browsing to the ease of ordering to the shock of ahead-of-schedule delivery to the convenience of returns, every touchpoint added up to one strong narrative about customer fixation.

Implementation Principle: Map out your entire customer journey so every touchpoint adds to earlier narrative building blocks, coalescing into a cohesive story that gets stronger with every interaction.

ETHICAL CONSIDERATIONS IN PERCEPTION HACKING

Since any great approach comes with great ethical responsibilities, perception hacking is no exception:

Experience Authenticity

Ethical perception hacking involves engineering real experiences, not inventing fictitious stories. Amazon's success was the result of actually providing on its customer obsession, not inventing a pretense that it did so. When customers told stories about Amazon's service, they were telling real stories, not recounting fabricated accounts.

Narrative Truthfulness

Whereas strategic in intent, ethical perception hacking has to create stories that are truly authentic brand realities. Amazon's customer obsession stories succeeded because they were essentially real, albeit strategically emphasized. Creating stories that have no basis in fact ultimately rebounds with a dramatic blow.

Value Reciprocity

Most sustainable is the way perception hacking brings real value exchange, where customers gain value so tremendous that they're worth telling stories for. Amazon's success in perception came from building experiences that actually made customers' lives better and caused narrative sharing to be a natural reaction to value delivered.

CONCLUSION: FROM NARRATIVE SUBJECT TO NARRATIVE MASTER

As we close out this chapter, keep in mind that the end purpose of perception hacking isn't to make people say different things- it's to make your brand into an active force shaping them instead of a passive recipient of customer stories.

When Amazon reached actual perception mastery, they didn't only get good word-of-mouth; they actually changed the way the whole retail category was being talked about. The discussion moved from products and price to experience and convenience. The customer relationship moved from transactional to emotional. The marketplace expectations moved forever in Amazon's favour.

This is the ultimate state of perception hacking triumph- where your brand isn't merely getting positive stories but actually shifts the entire category dialogue to terms that inherently benefit you, independent of competitor reactions.

The path to perception mastery is not just strategic- it involves a transformation of the way you think about your business. Instead of perceiving yourself mainly as a product or service maker, you need to rethink your role as a perception architect, meticulously designing every detail of the customer experience to create particular, strategic stories.

This transformation extends beyond communications or marketing groups- it has to reach product development, operations, customer support, and even finance. Each business choice is a story choice when it's seen from the point of view of perception hacking. It's not merely "How will it impact our metrics?" but "How will it impact the stories that our customers share?"

In Amazon's instance, this view resulted in supposedly counterintuitive business maneuvers which would have been spurned under orthodox management thinking. Their huge investments in customer support when rivals were slashing costs, their cannibalizing of their own business with new models, their focus on the long game when Wall Street was asking for short-term gains- all were vindicated by their awareness of narrative formation and the power of controlling perception over the long run.

The dividends of mastery of perception pay far more than short-term business dividends. They build compounding strengths that gather momentum over time:

Momentum of Story: As some perceptions gain purchase, they instill self-reinforcing loops that make each successive perception-forming experience stronger.

Insulation from Competition: Cemented perceptions build strong entry barriers, as rivals must not only defeat your product strengths but the deeply ingrained stories tied to your brand.

Premium Positioning: Fierce narrative control permits you to break free from commodity positioning and demand premium prices on the basis of stories around your brand and not simply functional benefits you provide.

Talent Magnetism: Companies with strong narrative presence attract and retain the best talent who desire to be identified with the stories your brand stands for in the market.

Decision Privilege: Most forcefully, narrative mastery gives you decision privilege- the power to make decisions that would be challenged or denied if tried by rivals without your story basis.

In the next chapter, we'll see how to turn this narrative superiority into sustainable competitive advantage through what I term "Expectation Setting"- deliberately setting the standards against which your whole category is measured.

As we go ahead, keep in mind these key questions:

1. What do your customers, right now, tell the stories about your company, and are these aligned to the stories with which you hope your business becomes associated?

2. What touches along your customer journey hold most narrative-generation opportunity, and how could you revamp them as opportunities to author more compelling, shareable storylines?

3. What kind of infrastructure do you have to capture customer tales systematically, amplifying and continuing them on the topic of your brand?

4. How could you break customer expectations in good ways that create stories consistent with your strategic positioning?

5. If your brand's destiny is being written in the stories customers tell, how intentionally are you designing the

experiences that will create those stories? And more importantly, what is the story you want them to tell?

Keep in mind: In the Perception Economy, what people think about you is more important than what actually is. The greatest businesses don't merely provide wonderful products and services- they design perceptions that build enduring competitive advantage through the stories customers naturally tell.

The question is not if your brand will create stories- every customer interaction will necessarily create stories. The only question is if you will leave those stories up to chance or methodically engineer them to propel your business. Perception hacking provides you with the structure to make certain that the stories being told about your brand are the stories you deliberately created instead of the stories that happened by chance.

As Jeff Bezos did with Amazon, by the time you become proficient in perception hacking, you not only compete in your space- you actually redefine how consumers experience, judge, and talk about your entire category, and have unparalleled control over the competitive landscape for years to come.

11

THE ECHO EXECUTION PLAN — STEP-BY-STEP ROADMAP FOR MARKET SUPREMACY

The difference between strategy and success is execution. This chapter provides a concrete, action-based roadmap for implementing the Echo Strategy framework for market dominance. Following this rational process will turn theoretical concepts into practical market dominance.

Phase 1: Building Foundations (Months 1-3)

Week 1-2: Intelligence Gathering on the Market

Begin with extensive market research that provides an information advantage

1. **Competitor Analysis Matrix:** Create a comprehensive database of each of the competitors' market positions, value propositions, pricing strategies, distribution networks, messaging styles, and customer opinions. Search for trends and holes that reveal opportunities in the marketplace. Note their strengths, weaknesses, and strategic tendencies from prior actions and messages.

2. **Customer Persona Engineering:** Develop 3-5 full customer archetypes out of psychographic profiles rather than simple demographics. Document their pain points, aspirations, objections, buying motivators, media usage, and decision-making process. Conduct thorough interviews with at least 20 customers per persona to validate your hypotheses and unearth gems.

3. **Trend Mapping:** Identify macro and micro trends that affect your sector. Examine patterns in close markets, which might foretell where your own markets are headed. Categorize trends as accelerating, stabilizing, or decelerating. Put ranges on impact timing and probability of disruption scope per trend, with particular attention to which trends might affect customer expectations or competitive environments.

4. **Ecosystem Analysis:** Map out the entire business ecosystem including suppliers, distributors, regulators, influencers, and complementary products or services. Identify power structures and leverage points of relations. Identify key decision-makers, gatekeepers, and influence nodes that can accelerate or slow down your market entry.

5. **Market Sentiment Analysis:** Use social listening tools to quantify the prevailing customer emotions, pain points, and unmet needs in your space. Identify recurring complaints, wish lists, and emotional drivers influencing buying behaviour. Create a heat map of sentiment trends across different customer segments and usage contexts.

This intelligence foundation is your directional compass,

informing all subsequent decisions and preventing costly directional mistakes.

Week 3-4: Echo Strategy Formulation

With your intelligence base in place, anchor your differentiation strategy:

1. Core Differentiation Workshop: Conduct a dedicated 2-day workshop with key stakeholders to establish your unique market position. The outcome should be a clear, compelling statement of how you differ in a manner that matters to customers. Try out multiple differentiation options against customer feedback, competitive environment, and internal capabilities to identify the strongest and most enduring position.

2. Reinvention of the Value Chain: Map your entire value chain from raw material to post-purchase support and identify opportunities for innovation, cost reduction, or experience enhancement at each step. Determine the 3-5 areas where reinvention would make the most evident customer impact and competitive advantage.

3. Minimum Viable Echo: Create the most basic, most summarized version of your differentiation that can be quickly created and implemented yet still produce customer resonance. This prevents scope creep and accelerates market feedback. Create a full specification for this MVP with explicit success criteria, resource requirements, and timeline milestones.

4. North Star Metrics: Develop 2-3 key performance indicators which will gauge your success at gaining market resonance and not vanity metrics that fail to measure real differentiation effect. Develop measurement methods and tracking mechanisms for them. Develop baseline expectations and milestone targets for the first 12 months of adoption.

5. Competitive Response Anticipation: Conduct a war-gaming exercise to project likely competitor reaction to your differentiation strategy. Develop contingency plans for various competitive scenarios, including price wars, me-tooing, FUD campaigns, and direct counterattacks.

Week 5-8: Resource Alignment

Prepare your organization to execute the echo strategy effectively:

1. Capability Gap Analysis: Honestly compare internal capabilities with strategic requirements. Enumerate existing strengths, weaknesses, and specific gaps to be bridged. Develop action plans for filling top; priority gaps through hiring, training, buying, or partnering.

2. Team Reframing: Reframe teams to customer journey experiences rather than functional groups. Break down silos that divide the customer experience. Apply cross; functional pods with responsibility for unique segments of the customer journey, with established ownership, authority, and accountability measures.

3. Budget Redistribution: Redistribution of funds from low; resonance projects to high; resonance opportunities. Apply zero; based budgeting with the necessity for justification of every spend against echo standards. Develop a formal resource allocation process with prioritization by differentiation effect rather than past custom.

4. Strategic Partnership Development: Find and initiate conversations with potential partners who can amplify your market echo. Rank the partners based on echo amplification potential. Design tailored partnership forms, value exchange arrangements, and governance frameworks that align incentives and protect your differentiation integrity.

5. Technology Stack Alignment: Align your technology stack to support your differentiation strategy. Decide on upgrades, replacements, or integrations that are needed to improve your differentiation delivery. Develop a phased implementation plan that disrupts least while impacting the most.

6. Knowledge Management System: Build a centralized market intelligence database, differentiation assets, and best practices. Implement processes for continuous updating, quality checking, and accessibility across the organization. Develop training programs that will enable effective utilization of these knowledge assets by everyone in the team.

Week 9-12: Setup of Echo Amplification System

Build the processes that will set your market differentiation in relief:

1. Customer Journey Engineering: Chart all the touchpoints along the customer journey, identifying key moments of truth where your differentiation must come alive. Create focused experience enhancements at each touchpoint. Create detailed blueprints for best; in; class experiences at each step, including scripts, visual cues, timing considerations, and emotional rewards.

2. **Message Consistency Framework:** Put in place comprehensive brand guidelines that ensure your differentiation is always communicated through all touchpoints, by all employees, at all times. Create accurate messaging templates, example libraries, and approval processes which ensure consistency while allowing context; appropriate customization.

3. **Echo KPI Dashboard:** Create a framework for tracking your differentiation effectiveness in real time with automated notifications on any measures below threshold levels. Create visualization tools where performance trends are immediately evident to decision; makers.

4. **Feedback Loop Implementation:** Put in place customer feedback collection systems and follow through on conclusions promptly. Introduce 48; hour response vehicles to close experience gaps. Set up closed; loop processes for feedback providers to learn about resulting activities.

5. **Innovation Pipeline Process:** Create a documented process for generating ideas, evaluating ideas, and executing ideas to reinforce your distinction. Create stage; gate metrics specifically designed to filter opportunities through differentiation effect.

Phase 2: Market Penetration (Months 4-6)

Week 13-14: Pilot Launch

Begin to create market resonance through a controlled launch:

1. **Echo Ambassador Program:** Find prospective customers who will become your champions. Develop special benefits for these early adopters for giving complete feedback and advocacy. Establish tangible onboarding, engagement, and reward programs that transform customers into zealous advocates.

2. **Minimum Viable Echo Launch:** Launch your core differentiation to this small audience with a focus on flawless execution rather than feature completeness. Implement heightened monitoring practices during this critical phase to identify and correct issues in real time. Create contingency plans for common failure modes.

3. **High-Touch Feedback Collection:** Implement formal qualitative feedback mechanisms like customer interviews, usage observation sessions, and in-depth experience surveys. Develop analysis frameworks that extract actionable insights from various sources of feedback.

4. **Rapid Iteration Process:** Establish 48; hour cycles of feedback and implementation, based on targeted, early adopter feedback. Give highest priority to fixes that further core differentiation. Create streamlined approval mechanisms that bypass normal bureaucratic paths for high; leverage improvements.

5. Consistency Monitoring Experience: Leverage mystery shopping and experience audit programs to maintain assurance that your differentiation is consistently delivered across all touchpoints. Establish minimum acceptability consistency measures and escalation protocols for addressing variation.

Week 15-18: Echo Amplification

Amplify your market presence in a deliberate way:

1. **Influencer Activation Strategy:** Activate and engage priority opinion leaders who truly connect with your differentiation. Construct relationship-based strategies rather than transactional sponsorships. Create customized activation plans for each high-priority influencer based on their specific audience, content orientation, and value alignment.

2. **Content Resonance Campaign:** Create useful content highlighting your differentiated method rather than announcing it. Highlight significant evidence rather than marketing claims. Construct a content matrix that offers comprehensive coverage of different persona needs, buying stage concerns, and objection handling requirements.

3. **Channel Optimization:** Double down on the channels whose performance metrics reflect your audience best and cut away non; performing channels. Create channel; specific renditions of your main message that stick to what they say but adapt for the quirks of each channel.

4. **Competitor Response Monitoring:** Implement systematic tracking of the ways in which competitors react

to your entry. Develop contingency planning for likely competitive countermoves. Develop a competitive intelligence fusion center that consolidates several sources of information for prompt pattern recognition.

5. Sales Enablement Program: Equip your sales team with the tools, training, and incentives that are specifically designed to communicate and tell your differentiation effectively. Develop role; playing scenarios, objection; handling scripts, and success stories that make your differentiation tangible to prospects.

Week 19-24: Systematic Scale-Up

Systematically scale up your market reach

1. Resonance Metric Validation: Inspect your North Star Metrics in depth to confirm your differentiation is gaining traction. Strategically make adjustments if resonance is lower than targets. Set up A/B testing initiatives to enhance lagging areas of your differentiation delivery.

2. Experience Consistency Audit: Implement formal testing processes to ensure that as you expand, your customer experience is consistent with your differentiation promise. Create standardized assessment criteria and scoring systems that objectively measure consistency across touchpoints, channels, and customer segments.

3. Resource Scaling Blueprint: Create a detailed milestone-based roadmap for scaling teams, infrastructure, and partnerships to accommodate growth without compromising your differentiation edge. Define clear trigger points that cause resource expansion before capacity starts to impact experience quality.

4. Echo Expansion Mapping: Identify adjacent markets or customer segments where your differentiation would be most resonant. Rank expansion opportunities by potential resonance. Set market entry plans for each top opportunity, as well as adaptations needed to your core differentiation.

5. Operational Excellence Program: Implement formal processes for refining efficiency, quality, and scalability of delivery of your differentiation. Implement process improvement programs that decrease costs without compromising experience quality.

Phase 3: Market Dominance (Months 7-12)

Week 25-32: Competitive Displacement

Begin actively taking market share:

1. Competitor Vulnerability Assessment: Identify specific competitors with vulnerabilities that your differentiation targets specifically. Develop targeted campaigns to claim their customers through direct comparative messaging. Create competitor; specific battle cards that equip your team with targeted information about competitive vulnerabilities and compelling counterarguments.

2. Switching Barrier Elimination: Create programs that systematically reduce financial, technical, psychological, and procedural barriers to switching to your product or service. Create transition support packages, compatibility solutions, and risk; reduction guarantees for different customer segments.

3. Objection Neutralization Framework: Create specific content, training, and sales approaches that overcome and counter common objections to your differentiated approach. Create a comprehensive objection library with tested responses validated through customer research.

4. Loyalty Architecture: Implement deterministic systems to lock in early customers as you grow, including recognition schemes, selective benefits, and active relationship management. Develop sophisticated segmentation strategies that can provide targeted loyalty experiences for different customer value segments.

5. Competitive Intelligence Network: Implement systematic processes for gathering, analyzing, and sharing competitive intelligence throughout your organization. Develop specific intelligence collection tasks for customer contact personnel.

Week 33-40: Category Definition

Shift from market player to market maker:

1. Thought Leadership Platform: Publish authoritative content that establishes your methodology as the new gold standard in your industry. Focus on educating rather than promoting to establish credibility. Develop a multi; year content plan that incrementally tackles major industry challenges through the lens of your differentiation.

2. **Standards Influence Campaign**: Target industry associations, regulatory bodies, and certifying bodies selectively to shape standards in line with your differentiation strategy. Identify pivotal committees, working groups, and points of influence where your presence could have the most impact.

3. **Market Education Initiative: Construct comprehensive** education programs that educate customers, partners, and even competitors to think about the category in terms that work necessarily to your advantage. Construct certification programs, training curricula, and educational material that make your business the first knowledge source in your category.

4. **Ecosystem Cultivation:** Actively create complementary products, services, and partnerships that complement your market position and create higher returns to scale. Create developer programs, partnership incentives, and resource sharing programs that encourage third-party investment in your ecosystem.

5. **Category Metrics Redefinition:** Work to redefine industry success metrics to metrics that serve your strategy. Publish research, case studies, and frameworks that establish new standards of measurement aligned with your differentiation.

Week 41-52: Echo Institutionalization

Make your market leadership stick for the long term:

1. **Culture Reinforcement Program:** Embracing systematic practices to make your internal culture fully aligned with

your market differentiation, like hiring, onboarding, recognition, and promotion standards. Create rituals, symbols, and stories that consistently reinforce your differentiation values.

2. **Operational Excellence System:** Develop advanced playbooks, training programs, and quality control processes that ensure repeatable delivery of your differentiated experience regardless of personnel or size changes. Implement continuous improvement practices focused mainly on differentiating delivery.

3. **Innovation Pipeline Management:** Create a structured process of ongoing innovation that maintains your lead in differentiation above eventual competitive response and market shift. Construct horizon scanning processes that identify early danger and opportunity.

4. **Talent Magnetism Strategy:** Position your company as the place to go for top talent in your market through thought leadership, culture branding, and career opportunity. Create distinctive employment experiences that align with your market differentiation.

5. **Strategic Narrative Evolution:** Evolve your market narrative in perpetuity in order to be current without trading differentiation integrity:

Develop regular narrative review cycles assessing market resonance and competitive positioning.

TOOLS AND TACTICS TO IMPLEMENT

The Weekly Echo Ritual

Introduce a devoted meeting that is exclusively for market differentiation:

- Align resonance measures against targets
- Deliver unfiltered customer feedback to the team in its entirety
- Identify differentiation delivery lapses
- Achieve tangible results where differentiation delivered tangible wins
- Create accountable owners out of to; do's that build your echo

The Echo Decision Filter

Create a simple yet powerful decision instrument to filter out all ventures:

1. Does this leverage our key differentiation?

2. Will customers notice and value this distinction?

3. Is this challenging for competitors to do?

4. Can we reliably deliver this at scale?

5. Does this create compounding advantage over time?

Any project that does not meet these standards should be revised or redesigned.

CONCLUSION: FROM STRATEGY TO DOMINANCE

This blueprint provides a step; by; step process for creating market dominance through disciplined execution of your differentiation strategy. No plan, however, ever survives contact with reality unscathed. The secret is not rigid adherence to this timetable but internalization of the underlying principles:

1. Start with deep market understanding

2. Develop genuine, substantive differentiation

3. Establish systems that consistently deliver your differentiated experience

4. Create amplification mechanisms that create market resonance

5. Grow deliberately without diluting your differentiation

6. Reinforce your echo consistently both inside and outside

The market leaders are not always those with the most resources or best ideas. They're those who execute their differentiation strategy with discipline, consistency, and determination.

Your echo execution plan must be a living document, regularly revisited and honed as you gather market feedback. The timeline may fluctuate, some tactics will evolve, but the entire strategy of building, amplifying, and institutionalizing your market differentiation remains the bedrock of enduring market dominance.

The journey from strategy to domination is hard but straightforward: understand your market, differentiate meaningfully, execute relentlessly. The Echo Execution Plan frames these maxims into a working guidebook. The rest is up to you.

12

THE FUTURE OF MARKETING ECHO — WHAT NEXT AFTER MARKET OWNERSHIP?

Market leadership is not an end point but a fleeting status that needs continuous reinforcement and change. Even the most effective echo strategies will eventually experience declining returns as markets develop, customer attitudes change, and competitors catch up. This chapter discusses the fundamental question that each market leader must ultimately face: what next after you've secured market ownership?

THE OWNERSHIP PARADOX

The biggest danger of sustained success usually arrives at the peak of your success. After you've achieved evident market dominance via your echo strategy, stronger forces start working against your sustained distinction:

1. **Competitive Convergence:** Your competitors observe,

imitate, and copy components of your differentiation, eventually depleting your distinctiveness in the marketplace.

2. **Customer Habituation:** Your previously novel differentiation becomes the norm, moving from a pleasant surprise to a minimum standard in customers' expectations.

3. **Organizational Complacency:** Internal momentum is dampened as the urgency that propelled your early market capture wears off into complacent leadership habits.

4. **Market Saturation:** Growth inevitably tapers off as you win over the most easily accessible segments of your target market, with only the more difficult; to; win; over segments remaining.

5. **Innovation Stagnation:** The company structures and processes that so flawlessly executed your initial differentiation can become the obstacles to creating the next breakthrough.

These forces set up what we refer to as the "Ownership Paradox"- the very success of your echo strategy holds the seeds of its ultimate decline. Recognizing and overcoming this paradox is the difference between enduring market leadership and another case study in fleeting success.

THE THREE PATHS FORWARD

When you've reached market ownership, there are three strategic routes to consider, each with unique strengths and weaknesses:

Route 1: Echo Deepening

Double down on your central differentiation and push it to more extreme depths that others cannot replicate without essential reinvention.

Key Strategies:

1. **Vertical Integration:** Have more control over your value chain to deliver greater differentiation. This could mean taking over suppliers, distribution channels, or complementary services providers.

2. **Experience Extremism:** Take your core differentiation to extremes that appear unreasonable to competitors but thrill your most loyal customers. If your differentiation is simplicity, become radically simple. If it's personalization, reach levels of customization that competitors deem economically irrational.

3. **Segment Specialization:** Find the customer segments that most appreciate your differentiation and develop hyper; specialized versions of your offering that meet their unique needs.

4. **Ecosystem Dominance:** Establish a holistic ecosystem of products, services, and alliances that generates increasing returns to scale and network effects for your core differentiation.

5. **Category Redefinition**: Proactively redefine category boundaries and assessment criteria to further highlight the dimensions where your differentiation is strongest.

CASE STUDY: APPLE'S ECOSYSTEM INTEGRATION

Apple's initial iPhone differentiation was around simplicity, design, and user experience. Instead of expanding into unrelated spaces, Apple doubled down on these points of differentiation by building an increasingly integrated network of devices and services. With each new product- from AirPods to Apple Watch- the core differentiation was extended while the entire ecosystem became more valuable. The use of custom silicon (M; series chips) is the final manifestation of this strategy, allowing Apple to control all facets of the user experience in a way that others cannot replicate without the same kind of vertical integration.

Difficulties with Echo Deepening:

- Danger of over differentiation to meet customer requirements
- Danger of returns on investment diminishing
- Resource requirements of vertical integration
- Lower agility as a result of added organizational complexity
- Susceptibility to disruptive innovations altering market fundamentals

Path 2: Echo Expansion

Path two is extending your differentiation to nearby markets and categories where your underlying strengths can build similar resonance.

Key Strategies:

1. **Market Adjacencies:** Identify near markets with similar need structures where your differentiation would resonate. Rank adjacencies by transferability of competitive advantages.

2. **Capability Extension:** Leverage your core capabilities in new ways that create distinct value in different market contexts. This often involves applying your methodology to solve different problems.

3. **Brand Architecture Evolution:** Develop a brand architecture that allows for application of your core differentiation across diverse offerings while maintaining coherent identity.

4. **Ecosystem Bridging:** Create connective tissue between previously separate ecosystems, positioning your offering as the essential integrative element.

5. **Differentiation Translation:** Translate your core differentiation into the language, requirements, and cultural setting of emerging markets without diminishing its fundamental nature.

CASE STUDY: AMAZON'S CATEGORY EXPANSION

Amazon's initial differentiation was convenience, choice, and customer focus in online book retailing. Instead of reinforcing this differentiation in books, Amazon deliberately moved into related retail categories while preserving its fundamental differentiation principles. This expansion ultimately reached outside of retail into entirely new markets such as cloud computing (AWS), where Amazon applied its operational prowess, scale benefits, and customer; focused innovation to a new setting. Every expansion supported and financed additional differentiation across all categories.

Challenges of Echo Expansion:

- Danger of differentiation dilution over too many markets
- Gaps in capability while entering new territory
- Confusion over the brand if growth does not have clear strategy
- Fragmentation of management attention
- Competition resistance from vested players in the new markets

Path 3: Echo Reinvention

The third approach is one where you disrupt your own success ahead of time by creating whole new differentiation strategies ahead of when the market forces your change.

Key Strategies:

1. Pre-emptive Disruption: Engineer your own disruption ahead of competition or startups doing it to you. This frequently means creating autonomous units with the clear mission to render your existing offerings irrelevant.

2. Differentiation Evolution: Evolve your differentiation deliberately along dimensions that continue to resonate with core customers while gaining traction with new segments.

3. **Strategic Discontinuity:** Intentionally break away from past methods when market indicators indicate declining resonance, even though current performance continues to be solid.

4. **Portfolio Approach:** Create a portfolio of differentiation strategies across levels of maturity so that there is a gradual realignment of priorities as markets mature.

5. **Capability Recombination:** Generate new differentiation by recombinations of existing capabilities in innovative combinations, producing innovations that stay anchored to your organizational DNA.

CASE STUDY: NETFLIX'S MULTIPLE REINVENTIONS

Netflix has consistently reimagined its differentiation in front of market forces. Its first differentiation was around convenient DVD; by-mail service without late fees. Before this model had a chance to mature, Netflix disrupted its own successful business by moving to streaming. When streaming became commoditized, Netflix reimagined itself once more as a content producer with data; driven original content. Each reinvention built on aspects of its prior differentiation while establishing completely new types of market resonance.

Challenges of Echo Reinvention:

- Cannibalization of successful existing businesses
- Resistance to change from within when the organization is performing strongly
- Maintaining organizational coherence throughout the transition
- Risk of losing core customers through reinvention
- Balancing resource allocation between present and future differentiation

THE ECHO EVOLUTION FRAMEWORK

Picking and choosing the right direction needs a disciplined approach to evolution. The Echo Evolution Framework offers this structure across five related phases:

Phase 1: Echo Horizon Scanning

Put in place systematic procedures for scanning for early indicators of differentiation degradation or new opportunity:

1. Resonance Metrics Analysis: Create advanced metrics that capture not only customer satisfaction but also the precise resonance of your differentiation. Monitor these metrics for early warning signs of waning effect.

2. Edge Exploration Program: Establish formal programs that examine the fringe of your marketplace, mapping emerging needs, technologies, and competitor actions that might affect your differentiation.

3. Customer Future-Casting: Use methodologies to forecast how customer needs and tastes will change, instead of merely reacting to immediate feedback.

4. Competitive Intent Analysis: Take it beyond monitoring current competitor behaviour to examining patterns that uncover their probable future strategies and differentiation strategies.

5. Technological Impact Mapping: Methodically analyze how new technologies might enhance, weaken, or reshape your existing differentiation strategy.

Phase 2: Evolution Portfolio Building

Develop a balanced portfolio of potential evolution routes at different levels of change size:

1. Differentiation Improvement Projects: Gradual enhancements of your existing differentiation to build further resonance with current customers.

2. Differentiation Expansion Projects: Utilization of your core differentiation across new customer groups, issues, or use cases.

3. Differentiation Transformation Ventures: More extreme reimagining's of your differentiation that stay connected to your core while generating significant new resonance.

4. Differentiation Revolution Experiments: Investigations of completely new differentiation methods that might ultimately supplant your existing echo strategy.

5. **Portfolio Governance Framework:** Establish clear processes for assessing, funding, and moving initiatives at each level, with suitable success metrics for each evolution scale.

Phase 3: Organizational Ambidexterity Building

Build the ability to leverage existing differentiation in parallel while venturing future possibilities:

1. **Structural Separation:** Establish clear organizational entities with respective cultures, metrics, and leadership for today's business optimization versus future differentiation building.

2. **Ring-Fencing Resources:** Create immune funding and talent pools for forward-looking initiatives which cannot be used for short-term priorities.

3. **Mechanisms for Integration:** Institute specific processes, roles, and forums that will facilitate knowledge transfers between exploitation and exploration units.

4. **Leadership Development:** Develop executives who possess the unique ability to execute current results alongside developing future capability.

5. **Cultural Balancing:** Foster organizational values and norms that respect both operating excellence and creative thinking and provide legitimate space for both philosophies.

Phase 4: Transition Management System

Establish advanced capabilities to manage the complicated transitions between differentiation strategies:

1. **Pacing Optimization:** Identify the optimal speed of transition according to market dynamics, competitive danger, and organizational preparedness.

2. **Narrative Evolution:** Develop engaging internal and external narratives that drive coherence between historical, contemporary, and prospective differentiation strategies.

3. Stakeholder Migration Planning: Create comprehensive plans to transition multiple stakeholders (customers, employees, partners) from existing to prospective differentiation models.

4. **Mechanisms of Investment Re-allocation:** Develop systematic frameworks for reallocating resources from losing to winning differentiation strategies at the ideal pace.

5. **Risk Balancing Framework:** Employ advanced risk management strategies that find the balance of risk between speeding up too soon and slowing up too late.

Phase 5: Renewal Institutionalization

Establish company systems that establish echo evolution as a sustainable competence:

1. **Differentiation Life Cycle Management:** Establish systematic processes for managing differentiation strategies from conception to maturity to elegant retirement.

2. **Echo Evolution Metrics:** Design organizational performance measures that reward effective differentiation evolution over and above business performance today.

3. **Insight System Development:** Develop systematic capabilities to collect, analyze, and respond to the customer, market, and competitive intelligence that fuels differentiation evolution.

4. **Dynamism in Capabilities:** Develop the organizational capacity to quickly create new capabilities and effectively phase out those no longer relevant to future differentiation requirements.

5. **Accelerating Learning**: Adopt mechanisms that shorten learning cycles around differentiation evolution, minimizing time and resources needed for effective transitions.

SUSTAINED ADVANCED ECHO STRATEGIES

In addition to the three foundational tracks, there are a number of advanced strategies that can be used to sustain market leadership across many evolution cycles:

Strategy 1: Differentiation Layering

Rather than replacing your current differentiation entirely, add complementary layers that create new forms of resonance while preserving existing ones:

1. **Base Layer Maintenance:** Preserve and incrementally improve the original differentiation that created your market success.

2. **Enhancement Layer Development:** Add new differentiation dimensions that enhance the value of your base differentiation for existing customers.

3. **Creation of Expansion Layers:** Develop differentiation aspects that expand your appeal to customer segments previously disinterested in your base differentiation.

4. **Incubation of Future Layers:** Try new and very different types of differentiation that might come to be core as base layers commoditize.

5. **Governance of Layers:** Establish transparent decision guidelines on whether to add, highlight, downplay, or phase out particular differentiation layers.

Case Study: Tesla's Differentiation Layering

Tesla started with a clear differentiation aimed at high; performance, desirable electric cars when EVs were regarded as underpowered and ugly. Instead of enhancing this differentiation, Tesla added layers methodically: autonomous driving, over; the; air software updates, energy ecosystem integration, and unique direct; to; consumer distribution. Each layer built new resonance while maintaining the value of earlier differentiators, making a constantly changing but consistent market position.

Strategy 2: Ecosystem Orchestration

Step out of owning a market into orchestrating an entire value ecosystem in which your differentiation serves as the key organizing principle:

1. **Platform Development:** Build technological, distribution, or relationship platforms that allow third parties to extend upon your differentiation.

2. **Complementor Cultivation:** Build out intentionally a network of partners that produce offerings to build upon and amplify the value of your core differentiation.

3. **Standard Setting:** Establish your approach as the de facto standard that others must adopt to participate effectively in the ecosystem.

4. **Value Flow Design:** Create economic and strategic structures that ensure appropriate value distribution among ecosystem participants while maintaining your central position.

5. **Ecosystem Governance:** Develop sophisticated mechanisms for directing ecosystem evolution while maintaining sufficient autonomy for participants.

Case Study: Salesforce's Ecosystem Orchestration

Salesforce progressed from merely providing differentiated CRM software to orchestrating a complete enterprise software system through its AppExchange platform, Trailhead education system, and Dreamforce community. This orchestration changed Salesforce from a market player to the central organizing entity in its space, building switching barriers and expansion opportunities much greater than its initial differentiation.

Strategy 3: Category Leadership Succession

Instead of being identified with one category, build the ability to systematically create, dominate, and then move beyond successive categories:

1. **Category Lifecycle Management:** Build skills in identifying and managing the stages of market and category maturity.

2. **Category Creation Capability:** Establish repeatable processes for finding and creating entirely new market categories where you can build fundamental differentiation.

3. **Trans; Category Brand Development:** Evolve your brand identity and associations to transcend particular categories and create a meta; position that enables movement between market spaces.

4. **Graceful Exit Mechanisms:** Establish means of transitioning out of declining categories without brand harm or undue resource waste.

5. **Institutional Memory:** Create mechanisms for retaining and utilizing the knowledge derived from past category leadership experience to new markets.

Case Study: Adobe's Category Leadership Succession

Adobe has managed through several category shifts- from desktop publishing software to tools for creative professionals to marketing technology platform to experience management system. Each shift capitalized on capabilities and market standing from earlier categories while creating leadership in completely new spaces. Adobe's brand and business model have followed suit, showing the unusual capability to lead consecutive categories versus rising and declining with a given market space.

THE SEVEN PRINCIPLES OF PERPETUAL ECHO

Companies that sustain market leadership through multiple cycles have seven underlying principles that extend beyond particular strategies:

Principle 1: Relentless Customer Truth; Seeking

Market leaders never cease to focus intensely on studying their customers even when performance today is good. They:

- Invest in advanced research techniques that uncover unexpressed needs
- Have direct executive contact with customers instead of depending on filtered reports
- Investigate non; customers as intensively as existing customers
- Listen particularly to those customers who are abandoning or diminishing interaction with their offerings
- Construct listening mechanisms that detect evolving needs prior to becoming voiced demands

Principle 2: Competitive Respect Without Paralysis

Successful market leaders strike a judicious balance in their competitive position:

- Research competitors in a systematic way without becoming reactive to all their moves

- Identify competitive threats early without reacting too emotionally or losing strategic direction
- Observe competitor innovations while preserving differentiation integrity
- Plan for competitive response when planning differentiation evolution
- Stay alert to emerging competition, not merely well; established competitors

Principle 3: Innovation Resource Discipline

Successfully evolving organizations have disciplined innovation resource practices:

- Invest innovation resources according to explicit portfolio models rather than political clout
- Insulate long; term innovation financing even in times of short-term performance difficulties
- Use demanding but suitable appraisal processes for initiatives in various evolution phases
- Match resource investments among enhancement, extension, and reinvention programs
- Develop distinct financing arrangements for sustaining present differentiation versus establishing new methods

Principle 4: Strategic Patience Coupled with Tactical Urgency

Market leaders that adapt successfully exhibit seemingly incompatible time orientations:

- Retain patience for the multi; year cycles needed for fundamental differentiation evolution
- Concurrently generate intense urgency in day; to; day implementation and learning cycles
- Avoid premature cessation of strategic directions due to early implementation issues
- Likewise avoid continuing with methods that have real evidence of decreasing resonance
- Create subtle appreciation of when to speed up and when to stay the course

Principle 5: Organizational Identity Flexibility

Sustainable market winners cultivate sophisticated practices for organizational identity:

- Develop values and sense of purpose extending beyond distinct differentiation strategies
- Develop narratives engaging past, current, and future differentiation strategies
- Craft visible processes for protecting essential elements of identity throughout changes
- Also, craft means for freeing up identity elements stifling essential evolution
- Forge leadership competency to navigate emotional and cultural aspects of identity evolution

Principle 6: Ecosystem Mindset

Long; term market leaders consider beyond their organizational horizons:

- Consider their success to rely on the well; being of a larger ecosystem of partners, suppliers, and complementors
- Create deep insight into the economic and strategic positions of major ecosystem participants
- Make choices that weigh near; term organizational gain against ecosystem long; term sustainability
- Foster the capacity for influencing ecosystem change without calling for direct control
- Identify when shifts in the ecosystem call for basic shifts in organizational positioning

Principle 7: Differentiation Humility

Most significantly, the organizations that endure market leadership through evolution cycles are humble regarding their differentiation:

- Accept that all differentiation advantages are transient, even in current strength
- Regularly question whether or not their approach continues to resonate, rather than expecting to remain relevant forever
- Establish psychological safety for internal voices questioning current differentiation orthodoxy
- Learn history in the market so that they know how once; unassailable differentiation advantages dissipated
- Balance confidence in current approach with openness to fundamental reconsideration

CONCLUSION: THE ULTIMATE ECHO STRATEGY

The final test of echo strategy success is not dominance in the market at a given moment, but the creation of an organization that can continuously evolve differentiation. In an era of speeding change, the capacity to methodically build, deploy, exploit, and then move beyond sequential differentiation advantages becomes the meta; capability that enables long; term market leadership.

The future of marketing echo does not lie in discovering a single ideal differentiation strategy, but in creating companies with the strategic foresight, cultural flexibility, and operational agility to constantly refresh their market relevance. The firms that excel at this evolutionary competence escape the classic trajectory of corporate boom and bust, accomplishing something much more valuable than fleeting ownership of the marketplace: the ability for perpetual relevance.

The journey is tough. It involves juggling opposing imperatives, taking tough decisions when triumph still looms within reach, and forging organizational competencies that do not yet seem essential. But for those leaders with the foresight to gaze beyond market supremacy now to the question of "what next?", the payoff is remarkable- enduring leadership through several market cycles and the building of companies that do not merely thrive in the short term but survive substantively.

The echo never stops; it either evolves or fades. The choice is yours.